تحـرّي المطـر
Yearning for Rain

شادن البليهد ومديحة صباني
Shadin Albulaihed and Madiha Sebbani

Yousef Jaha has emerged as a prominent contemporary artist who contributed significantly to the Saudi art scene, leaving an indelible mark on the local art community. His influence extends beyond the canvas into Saudi Arabia's art education field. He dedicated many years of his career to teaching before retiring to be a full-time artist. His multifaceted roles as an artist and educator underscore his comprehensive impact on the local art scene. In the early 1970s, Jaha redirected his path toward the arts and enrolled at the Institute of Art Education in Riyadh, Saudi Arabia.

This exhibition is a unique exploration of the artist's dual fascination with his natural surroundings and the architectural tapestry that defines his environment. *Yearning for Rain* acts as a bridge between Jaha's figurative work of urbanism and the layers of expressionist and lyrical abstraction. In his abstract paintings, his depictions of rainy clouds center an expansive imaginary sky, serving as the artist's signature composition and offering a singular perspective and pictorial direction that transcends symbolism. His compositions create a spiritual fusion of fundamental elements of nature and a harmonious interplay between human creation and the natural world. This exhibition

يوسـف جاهـا هـو فنـان معاصـر بـارز قـدّم الكثير للمشـهد الفني السعودي، تاركاً خلفه أثراً خالداً في المشهد الفني في السـعودية، فتأثيره غير محصور فـي فنـه، بـل انعكـس علـى حرصـه بتعليـم الفن. ففـي أوائـل السـبعينيات عاد يوسـف إلى شـغفه الأول وهو الفن، والتحق بمعهـد التربية الفنية في الريـاض، المملكة العربية السـعودية، وكرّس نفسـه سـنوات عديدة للتدريـس قبل أن يتفرغ لممارسـة الفن بعـد التقاعد.

يكشـف معرض «تحرّي المطر» شغف الفنان بالطبيعـة مـن حولـه، بالإضافة رسـمه النسـيج المعمـاري الـذي يعكس بيئتـه، ويُعدّ جسـراً يربط بيـن أعمالـه التـي تصـور البيئـة الحضريـة التـي لحقـت بها طبقـات التجريد التعبيـري والتجريد الإيقاعـي. فالغيـوم الماطـرة التـي تلامـس زرقـة السـماء فـي لوحات جاهـا توحـي بمنظـور فريد وتصويـري يتخطّى حدود الرسـم، وتتمثّـل بصمته وأسـلوبه فـي الرسـم وتعكـس التناغم بين البشـر والطبيعـة، وتدمـج بيـن العناصـر الأساسـية للطبيعـة وعلم النفس؛ لذا يأتي المعرض مسـلطاً الضوء علـى لوحاته التي تُصور المناظـر الطبيعية بأسـلوب واقعي إلى جانب لوحاته التجريدية التي تشـكل فيهـا السـحابة الممطـرة توقيعـاً حاضـراً يرسـم آفاقـاً علـى أعماله.

يُجسـد معرض «تحـرّي المطر» تطور أسـلوب جاها التشـكيلي، فقـد احتوت لوحاته السـابقة على مناظر حضرية من مسقط رأسه -مكة-، ومع تطور ممارسـاته تجـرّدت لوحاتـه مـن الطبيعـة كمناظر، ليدمـج التـلال والسـماء والجبـال بالألـوان فكوّنت إيحـاءات إيقاعيـة مسـتوحاة مـن تفاصيـل دقيقة للطبيعـة مـن حوله.

بدأ الفنان يوسـف جاهـا الفـن التجريدي في أواخـر التسـعينيات، واسـتمر في تطوير نفسـه في العقديـن الأخيريـن في مرسمِه في مكة إلى يومنا هـذا. يُعـدّ أسـلوب الفنـان فـي لوحاته مزجـاً بين الواقـع والتجريـد، فتفاصيـل كل لوحـة هـي صـور مجـردة مثـل قطـع الأحجيـة التـي تشكّل صورة عن الحقيقـة والواقـع، ويتجلى هذا الأسـلوب بدءاً مـن الاستكشـافات التصويريـة للمناظر الطبيعيـة والمعماريـة والحضرية في مكة، كمـا تتناغم أفكاره مـع فنانيـن آخريـن مـن نفـس جيلـه فـي العالـم العربـي مثل مصطفـى حفيـظ ومحمـد رومـان عطاالله.

كما اسـتفاد الفنان من خبرته الواسعة كمعلّم للفنون، وكمراقب لتعابير وأسـاليب رسـم طلابه في المرحلـة الابتدائيـة للطبيعة التي تتضمـن الغيوم الماطـرة، والتـي تُعـد رمز إلهـام للأطفـال ومصدراً للحياة، كل هـذه العوامل أصبحت مهامّ موضوعية في أعماله.

ففـي تشـكيل الغيـوم والسـماء، يضع الفنان نفسـه ضمن التجريـد الكامل للأشـكال والألوان مع الحفـاظ علـى أسـلوبه التصويـري المميـز، وبمزجه للغيوم في لوحاته يسـلّط الضوء على الأفق والجزء العلوي من اللوحة، واختياره المتعمد لرسم جمالية السـماء فـي لوحاته يخلق سـرداً مرئياً يمتـد إلى ما هـو أبعد من مجرد الرسـمة.

سـلك الفنان يوسـف جاها خطأ في أسـاليب المدرسـة التعبيرية التجريدية في العقد الثاني من القرن الحادي والعشـرين، حيث ركز بشكل كبير على اكتشـاف ألـوان تعبر بشـكل دقيـق عـن العواطف،

His style spontaneously developed into abstract expressionism in the 2000s as he heavily focused on uncovering colors that accurately express emotion. Jaha sees his entire practice as a representation of nature and people. Through his work, Jaha often creates a spiritual fusion of the fundamental elements of nature and psychology while attempting to represent these subjects using the simplest shapes, forms, and colors. In addition to his exploration of various styles and themes, Jaha's color palette is notably rich in earthy tones and nature-inspired hues. His use of shades of greens, oranges, and blues reflects his deep connection to the natural world and its diverse elements. These earthy colors not only evoke the landscapes and environments he portrays but also add layers of symbolism and depth to his works. Through the careful selection of colors, Jaha infuses his compositions with a sense of vitality and harmony, while also conveying the complexity and diversity of human emotion and experience. His most recognizable style is evident in his chromatic color palette, his composition of segmented planes, and his careful reduction of the subject.

Jaha's studio practice is characterized by a rich and diverse exploration of materials and time periods. Employing different canvases, colors, and tools, he imparts a unique touch across four distinct styles within his paintings, which are figurative, calligraphic, abstract, and expressionist. Early on, Jaha's practice involved calligraphy; he incorporated Arabic letters and experimented with seven calligraphic styles. This art form evolved as he witnessed his father's craftsmanship in creating student boards for elementary schools in Makkah. Jaha was immersed from a young age in the craft that would later come to define his path.

Another dimension of Jaha's work involves architectural documentation as he captured the highlights the artist's figurative and abstract paintings, the rainy cloud is a present signature, drawing the horizons within his abstract works.

Yearning for Rain traces the evolution of Jaha's stylistic approach. Where earlier paintings depicted natural landscapes from his hometown Makkah in pictorial detail, his work now abstracts those elements. Hills, skies, and mountains are translated into an essential color palette and lyrical simplistic forms. These distilled elements reflect Jaha's environment and are inspired by close-up details of nature and emotional expression.

Jaha began experimenting with abstract styles in the late 1990s and spent the last two decades expanding his practice from his studio in Makkah and continues to do so today. In his paintings, Jaha merges reality with abstraction; detailing singular abstract images like puzzle pieces that together form a cohesive whole. This theory unfolds starting with figurative explorations of Makkah's architecture, urban landscapes, and nature. His thoughts resonated with artists of his generation across the Arab world, such as Mustafa Hafid and Mohamed Romain Ataallah.

Jaha's extensive experience as an art educator had a large influence on his practice. He drew inspiration from his elementary students' simple and youthful expressions and the common techniques portraying nature including the raining clouds; a symbol of inspiration and life. Within Jaha's portrayal of the clouds and sky, he embraced the full abstraction of forms and colors as he maintained a singular perspective and pictorial direction. By integrating clouds into his paintings, he indirectly places emphasis on the horizon and the upper part of the canvas. This deliberate choice contributes to the overall atmospheric quality of his works, creating a visual narrative.

وتعتبـر ممارسـته الفنيـة بأكملهـا تمثيـلاً للطبيعة، والتي تشـمل البشر.

يقـوم جاهـا فـي كثير مـن الأحيان مـن خلال أعماله، بخلق اندماج روحي بين العناصر الأساسـية للطبيعة وعلـم النفس، ويحاول تمثيل الموضوعات باستخدام أشـكال وألوان غير معقدة، بالإضافة إلى استكشافه أساليب ومواضيع متنوعة.

تتميـز أعمـال جاهـا بألـوان غنيـة مسـتوحاة مـن درجـات ألـوان الطبيعـة وتداخلاتهـا، ويعكس باستخدامه للّون الأخضر والبرتقالي والأزرق ارتباطه العميـق بالطبيعة وعناصرها المتنوعة؛ هذه الألوان لا تسـتحضر فقط المناظر الطبيعيـة والبيئات التي يصورهـا، بـل تضيـف إلـى أعماله رمزيـة ومجازاً، كمـا يُضفي علـى تكوينـات اللوحة شـعوراً بالحيوية والانسـجام من خلال اختيـاره الدقيق للألوان، ومن خـلال استكشـافاته يُلحـظ اسـتحضاره للعديد من المشـاعر الإنسـانية، وفـي أسـلوبه المتميـز يتجلـى اسـتخدامه للألوان وحرصـه علـى ترتيـب عناصـر اللوحة وتنسيقها وتناوله الدقيق والسلس لموضوع العمـل الفني.

تتميّـز ممارسة يوسـف جاها الفنية باستكشاف ثـري للمـواد والفترات الزمنيـة، مسـتخدماً مختلف اللوحـات والألـوان والأدوات، مضيفاً بذلك لمسـته المميـزة علـى اللوحـات التي تظهـر أربعة أسـاليب مختلفـة، ويتضمّـن أحـد أسـاليب فنـه المبكر فن الخط، واسـتخدامه للحروف العربية وتجربة سبعة أنماط من الخط، فقربه من والده ومراقبته له وهو يعمـل علـى مجـلات الحوائـط المكتوبة يدوياً في مكـة المكرمة، كان سـبباً في تطوره بهذا الأسـلوب؛ ويتضمن الأسـلوب الآخر لجاها التوثيـق المعماري، فيصور منازل مكة المكرمة ويسـتوحى مشـاهد من طفولته للكعبة المشـرفة والطبيعـة المحيطة بها، فشغفه بالبيئة المعمارية أثر على حياته الشخصية، فقد نشـأ وترعرع فـي بيئة عائليـة اجتماعية يعيش فيهـا والداه مـع الأعمـام والأقارب، فـكان في أحد هذه المنازل أول اسـتوديو للفنان يوسـف جاها.

In his latest artistic endeavor, Jaha introduces a vibrant geometric precision across large canvases defined by intense, bright colors. Rainy clouds are persistent motifs, merging spontaneity with the structured arrangement of colors, forms, and compositions. Reflecting on his varied artistic movements, Jaha states:

"Putting in order and organizing excludes spontaneity, but there is always spontaneity in organization."

Throughout Jaha's career, he has made significant contributions to the Saudi art scene and has had a lasting impact on the local art community. As both an artist and educator, Jaha's multifaceted roles underscore his vast influence. His exploration of natural surroundings and architectural tapestries result in a body of work that transcends symbolism and offers a unique perspective on the fusion of nature and psychology. Jaha's artistic journey, marked by experimentation, international influences, and a dedication to capturing the essence of his environment, cements his legacy as a prominent figure in the Saudi art scene.

مـن خـلال خوضـه فـي التجريـد التعبيـري والإيقاعـي، يرى الفنان أن هذا الاهتمـام كان عفوياً قبل مسـيرته التعليمية وبعدها، فمن خلال مراقبته للأعمـال الفنيـة التـي يصنعهـا طُلابه فـي المرحلة الابتدائية وتعمقه فـي التفاصيل التصويرية لتجاربه وعواطفـه وتأثيراته، رسـم جاها الكثير من الأشـكال التجريديـة والبورتريـه والطبيعـة التـي تظهـر فيها الغيـوم الماطرة على القماش والورق، وهو أسـلوب مميز يعكس جوهر الفنان وخياله الواعي واللاواعي.

تأثـر الفنان بالفنانيـن التجريدييـن وتعبيراتهم الفنيـة كثيراً خـلال زيارتـه المتاحـف العالميـة والمشـاركة فـي المعـارض، حيث أعجب بأعمـال الفنـان مـارك روثكو فـي متحـف تيت مـودرن في لندن، بل ودرس طريقته في الرسم ومنهجه المادي فـي التجريـد التعبيري.

كما تعـرَّف علـى مُختلف أدوات الرسـم، منها الـورق المقوى الذي يمثِّل بدايـة مرحلة جديدة في فنِّه، والفرش الحادة والناعمة، ويسـتخدم أسـلوب سـفوماتو ويمزج الألوان بسلاسـة، ويحسن الأشكال غير المتبلورة.

وفي أحدث محاولاتـه الفنية قدَّم جاها لوحة كبيـرة تميـزت بالدقـة الهندسـية والألوان القوية والمشـرقة، كما يعتبر الغيوم الماطرة عنصراً مهماً فـي لوحاتـه، فهـي تدمـج العفويـة بالترتيـب فـي الألـوان والأشـكال والتراكيـب الفنية، ويعلـق جاها ببلاغـة على أسـاليبه الفنيـة المتنوعـة قائلاً:

«النظام ينافي العفويـة، ولكنها دائماً ما تكون حاضرةٌ فيه».

قـدم جاهـا مسـاهمات كبيـرة فـي المشـهد الفني السـعودي خلال مسـيرته الفنية، وكان له تأثير دائم على المجتمـع الفني المحلي. وبصفته فناناً ومعلماً أكـدت أدواره المتعـددة على تأثيره الواسـع. يؤدي استكشـافه للبيئة الطبيعية والمعماريـة المحيطة بـه إلى مجموعـة من الأعمـال التي تتجـاوز الرمزية وتقدم منظـوراً فريداً حول اندمـاج الطبيعة وعلم

intricacies of Makkah's houses, inspired by his childhood experience of viewing the Holy Kaaba and the surrounding landscapes. His connection to the architectural environment is also derived from his personal history. He grew up in a communal family setting where interconnected houses united parents, uncles, and other relatives. One of these houses was Jaha's very first studio space.

Venturing into calligraphy, expressionism, and lyrical abstraction, Jaha sees his practice as something that occurred spontaneously before and after his teaching career.

As he observed the artworks of his elementary school students and delved into figurative details of his own experiences, emotions, and influences, he painted abstract forms on canvas and paper with identifiable yet enigmatic portraits and landscapes, which included recurring rain clouds—a signature element reflecting the essence of Makkah and his conscious and unconscious imagination.

Jaha's continuous dedication to learning and exploring works of international artists enabled him to broaden his knowledge and expand his artistic practice. This dedication also allowed him to embrace the influence of abstract artists and their distinctive styles. A notable example is when Jaha encountered the work of Mark Rothko at Tate Modern in London. Impressed by the simplicity of his work, Jaha studied his painting style and material approach.

Through experimentation with various mediums, including cardboard, Jaha creates unique compositions while remaining true to his artistic vision. His experimentation allowed him to discover the sfumato technique to seamlessly blend colors into amorphous forms, which became a signature element of his recognizable style.

النفس، لذا تميزت رحلتـه الفنية بالتجربة والتأثيرات الدوليـة والتفانـي في التقـاط جوهر بيئتـه، وعززت إرثه كشـخصية بارزة في المشـهد الفني السعودي.

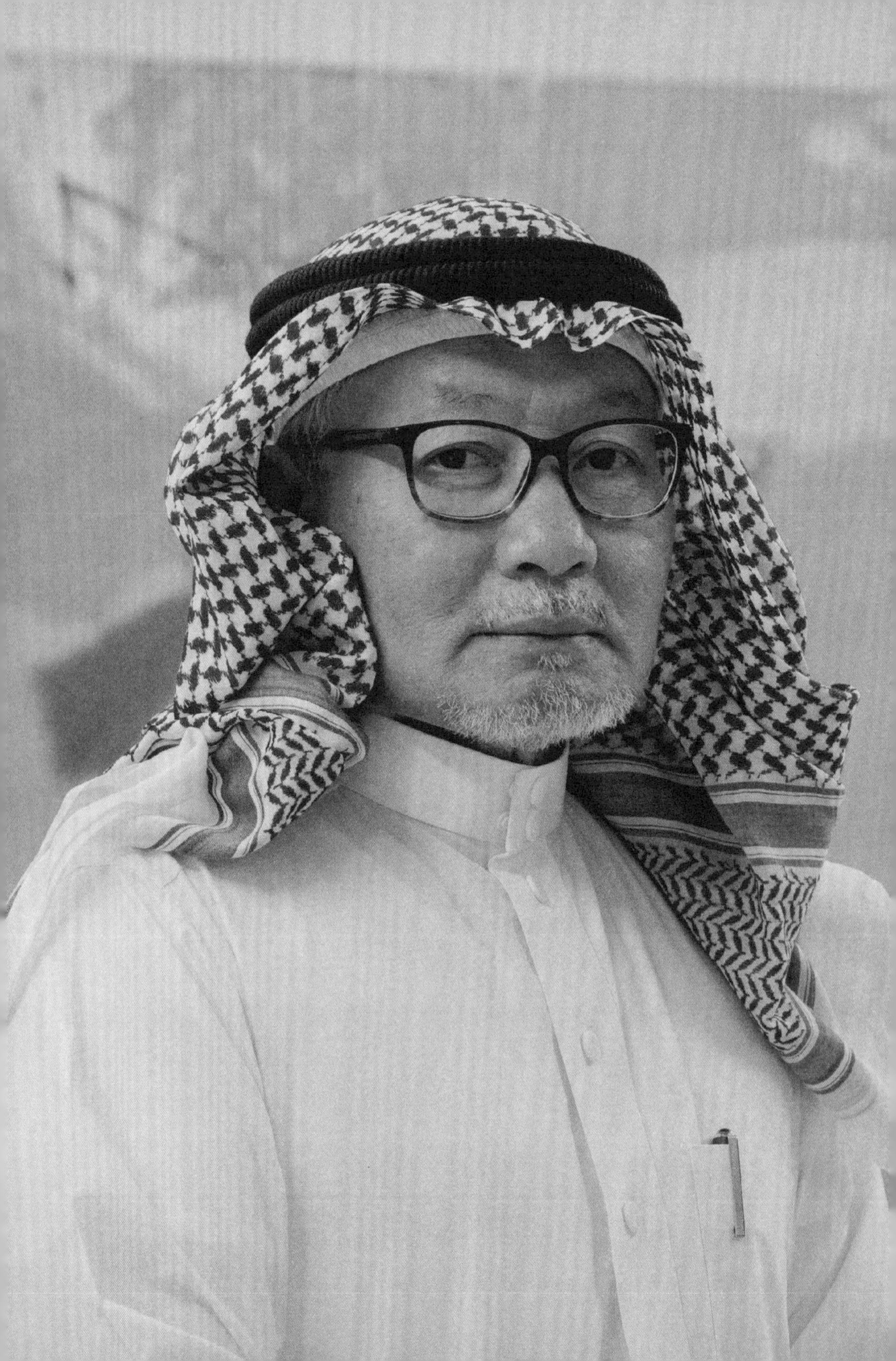

يوســف جاها
Yousef Jaha

شادن البليهد ومديحة صباني
Shadin Albulaihed and Madiha Sebbani

Growing up in a household brimming with creativity, Yousef Jaha was captivated by his father's calligraphy, sparking a deep-seated love for art that would shape his future endeavors. His childhood experiences, from drawing on the walls of his house to observing his father's calligraphic work, laid the foundation for his devotion to art. After briefly studying at Aramco and contemplating a specialization within the oil industry, Jaha realized that this path did not resonate with his true passion, prompting him to shift his career toward the pursuit of art.

In 1972, Jaha enrolled in the Institute of Art Education in Riyadh. During this time, he encountered fellow artists like Ahmed Monshi, Khalil Hassan Khalil, and Othman Alkhuzaim, kindling a creative camaraderie that endured throughout his career. He later became an art teacher at the King Faisal Model School in Makkah. In 1983, Jaha graduated with a degree in arts from Umm Al-Qura University. After his studies, he launched his career by participating in exhibitions in the same year, such as the group exhibition at The Golden Sail Gallery in Kuwait.

نشأ الفنان يوسـف جاهـا في بيـت ملـيء بالإبداع، أسره الخط العربي من ممارسة والده وذلك ما أوقد فيـه حبّاً عميقاً للفن وولّد لديه شـغفاً شـكّل مسـار مسـتقبله. فقد وضعت تجاربه في الطفولة الأسس لتفانيه في الفن، بدايةً من الرسـم على جدران منزله إلـى مراقبتـه جهود والده فـي الخط العربـي. وبعد فترة قصيرة من الدراسـة في أرامكـو ، أدرك جاها أن هذا السعي لا يتفق مع شغفه الفني الحقيقي، الأمر الذي دفعه لتغيير مسـاره نحو السـعي وراء الفن.

التحـق يوسـف جاهـا بمعهـد التربيـة الفنية فـي الرياض عـام 1972م، وخلال تلـك الفترة التقى بزملائه الفنانين، منهم الفنان أحمد منشـي وخليل حسـن خليـل وعثمـان الخزيـم، وقـد وضعـت تلك الفترة الأساس لالتزامه بمسيرته الفنية، حيث أصبح معلمـاً للفن في مدرسـة الملك فيصـل النموذجية فـي مكة المكرمة. تخرج جاهـا من جامعة أم القرى في عـام 1983م لتنطلـق بعدها مسـيرته المهنية في المعـارض الفنية، مثـل المعـرض الجماعي في غاليري الشـراع الذهبي فـي الكويت.

الفنـان يوسـف جاهـا هـو أحـد روّاد الفـن في المملكـة الذيـن يـروون لنـا من خـلال فنونهـم قصة تتجاوز الحدود الجغرافية وتتعمق في النفس البشرية.

transitioning from teaching to becoming a full-time artist in the early 2000s. He took part in international exhibitions such as the 8th Cairo International Biennale in Egypt (2001) and Edge of Arabia Exhibition in the United Kingdom (2008). Jaha's artworks were acquired by local and international collections including the Jordan National Gallery of Fine Arts in Amman, Jordan, and King Fahd International Airport in Riyadh, Saudi Arabia. His other notable awards include the Beautifying Holy Makkah Prize, Saudi Arabia (2010), Al-Danah Award for the 25th Art Exhibition, Kuwait (1997); Saudi Color Competition, Saudi Arabia (1992 and 1997); Golden Palm Award, Saudi Arabia (1989).

Jaha's many accomplishments, and significant contributions to the cultural landscape, both nationally and internationally, situate him as an important figure in Saudi art history.

تطورت أسـاليب جاها الفنية على مر السـنين، واعتمـدت بشـكل كبيـر علـى العناصـر الداخليـة والخارجيـة للطبيعـة البشـرية، فقـد كانـت أعمالـه الأولى مصوّرة بأسلوب واقعي؛ وتضمنت البورتريهات والمناظر الطبيعية والطبيعة السـاكنة، ثم توسعت معرفتـه بحـركات الفـن، أثنـاء دراسـته فـي معهـد التربية الفنيـة، حيـث صـوّر شـوارع مكـة المكرمـة وعمرانهـا، وجـرب أسـاليب متنوعـة منهـا الرسـم المعمـاري والتجريـدي والتعبيري، وكذلـك الحروفي وهو الأسلوب الذي يستخدم أشكال الحروف العربية والخـط العربي فـي التكويـن الفني.

تأثر الفنان بأسـاليب عالمية مختلفة واسـتمد إلهامه مـن رواد الفـن التجريـدي كمـا اتبـع غريـزة مشـتركة بين أبرز الفنانين العالميين ودرس أعمالهم واسـتخدمها كمراجع له. تكشـف رحلة يوسف جاها الفنيـة عن نفسـها بترتيـب زمني عكسـي، بـدأ من مشاركته الأخيرة في معرض «من حولهم» الجماعي في الرياض، المملكة العربية السـعودية الذي شـارك فيه روّاد الفن السـعودي من تنسـيق معهد مسك للفنـون في عام 2023م. وأقـام معرضه الفردي في عـام 2019م في معرض مونو فـي الرياض، المملكة العربيـة السـعودية، مؤكـداً بذلك تفانيـه في التطور الفنـي، إذ شـكّل هـذا المعـرض دليلاً علـى الطبيعة المسـتمرة لعملـه الفنـي، حيـث جـذب الجمهـور بمزيجـه الفريد بيـن الأصالة والألـوان الهادئة.

وفـي عـام 2017م وصلت رحلـة جاهـا الفنية إلـى ذروة جديدة بالتعاون مع الفنـان أحمد فلمبان في معرض ثنائي سـلّط الضـوء على وجـوه العمق فـي التعبير الفني وتنوعـه في حافـظ غاليري جدة، المملكة العربية السـعودية، الأمر الـذي أظهر الوفرة المسـتمرة في استكشافه الإبداعي،

بالعـودة إلـى أوائل الألفيـة الميلاديـة، أصبحت أعمـال جاها جـزءاً أساسـياً من المجموعـات المحلية والعالمية، بدءاً من مشاركته في البينالي الدولي الثامن في القاهرة (2001م)، إلى معرض Edge of Arabia في لنـدن (2008م).

Through his work, Jaha weaves a narrative that transcends geographical boundaries and delves deep into the human psyche. His early works were created in a realistic style and his subjects included portraits, landscapes, and still life. During his studies at the Institute of Art Education, he broadened his knowledge of art movements and depicted the streets and architecture of Makkah. He experimented with styles including figurative architectural painting, hurufiyya (a style that uses Arabic letter forms and calligraphy in a composition), lyrical abstraction, and expressionism.

International art movements influenced Jaha's studio practice. Inspired by pioneering abstract artists, he followed a common thread among world-renowned artists; studying and emulating their works as references.

Jaha has exhibited extensively, his latest group exhibition was in 2023 at Misk Art Institute titled *Echoing the Land*, featuring pioneering Saudi artists in Riyadh, Saudi Arabia. In 2019, his most recent solo exhibition *Mada* took place at Mono Gallery in Riyadh, Saudi Arabia, and reaffirmed his dedication to his artistic evolution. This exhibition served as a testament to the enduring nature of his artistic expression, captivating audiences with his unique blend of calm colors and originality.

In 2017, Jaha collaborated with artist Ahmed Felemban for a dual exhibition at Hafez Gallery, Jeddah, Saudi Arabia. This joint venture spotlighted the diversity and depth within his artistic expression as well as the continued richness of his creative exploration.

In 1979, Jaha received the first prize at *The Third General Art Exhibition* by the General Presidency of Youth Welfare in Riyadh, Saudi Arabia, marking a turning point in his career as well as the beginning of his enduring impact on the Saudi art scene. He began

إن قرار جاها بالانتقال من التدريس إلى أن يصبح فناناً متفرغاً بالكامل، يعكس تفانيه ويمثل فصلاً مهماً في رحلته الفنية، وقد حصل في أواخر الثمانينيات على الاعتراف الدولي؛ فحاز على جائزة "النخلة الذهبية Golden Palm Award في دورتها الأولى لمجلس تعاون دول الخليج في الرياض (1989م)، كما شارك في عام 1993م في البينالي الآسيوي الرابع في بنغلاديش، هذه المشاركات في أواخر الثمانينات لم تُسهم فقط في اكتسابه الشهرة الدولية، بل عرضت عمق تعبيره الفني على المسرح العالمي.

حاز جاها على تقدير كبير وجوائز مهمة طيلة مسيرته الفنية، ففي عام 1979، حقق مرحلة حاسمة بفوزه بالجائزة الأولى في "المعرض الفني العام الثالث" في الرياض، الذي نظمته الرئاسة العامة لرعاية الشباب؛ أكد هذا التقدير المبكر موهبة جاها الاستثنائية وتفانيه الثابت في الفن، وفي عام 2010م، أضاف جاها جائزة مرموقة أخرى إلى إرثه الفني بحصوله على جائزة تجميل مكة المكرمة، مؤكداً الأثر المستمر لمزيجه الفريد من الألوان الهادئة والتعبير الأصيل.

هذه الجوائز لا تُؤكد قدرةَ جاها الفنية فحسب، بل تسلط الضوء أيضاً على إسهاماته الملموسة في المشاهد الثقافية على الصعيدين المحلي والدولي.

وفي عام 2017م وصلت رحلة جاها الفنية إلى ذروة جديدة بالتعاون مع الفنان أحمد فلمبان في معرض ثنائي سلّط الضوء على وجوه العمق في التعبير الفني وتنوّعه في حافظ غاليري جدة، المملكة العربية السعودية، الأمر الذي أظهر الوفرة المستمرة في استكشافه الإبداعي.

حاز جاها على تقدير كبير وجوائز مهمة طيلة مسيرته الفنية. ففي عام 1979م، حقق مرحلة حاسمة بفوزه بالجائزة الأولى في المعرض الفني العام الثالث في الرياض من تنظيم الرئاسة العامة لرعاية الشباب، ليؤكد هذا التقدير المبكر على موهبة

جاهـا الاسـتثنائية وعلى تفانيـه في الفـن، وبالعودة إلى أوائل الألفية الميلاديـة، أصبحت أعمــال جاهـا جـزءاً أسـاسياً مـن المجموعات المحلية والدولية، بـدءاً مـن مشـاركته في بينـالي القاهـرة الـدولي الثامـن في مصر عـام 2001م، إلى معـرض «Edge of Arabia» في لنـدن عـام 2008م، واقتنيت أعماله الفنية من خـلال مجموعات محليـة ودولية بمـا فيها المتحف الوطنـي الأردنـي للفنون الجميلـة في عمّـان، الأردن ومطار الملك فهد الدولي في الرياض، المملكة العربية السـعودية؛ كمـا تشـمل الجوائـز البـارزة التـي حصل عليهـا جائـزة تجميل مكـة المكرمـة 2010م وجائزة الدانة للمعرض الفني الخامس والعشرين في الكويت 1997م ومسـابقة ملون السـعودية، المملكة العربية السعودية في العامين 1992 و1997م؛ وجائزة النخلة الذهبية في المملكة العربية السـعودية 1989م.

هــذه الجوائـز لا تؤكد قـدرة جاهـا الفنيـة فحسـب، بـل تُسـلط الضـوء أيضاً على إسـهاماته الملموسـة، وتؤكد مكانته كشـخصية رائـدة ومهمة في تاريـخ الفـن في المملكـة العربية السـعودية.

التسلســل الزمني لســيرة الفنــان
Artist Timeline

Yousef Jaha was born in Makkah, Saudi Arabia	**1955**	ولــد الفنــان يوســف جاهــا فــي مكــة المكرمــة، المملكة العربية السعودية.
Art was incorporated into the general education curriculum across Saudi Arabia	**1958**	دُمج الفن في المناهج الدراسية لجميع المستويات في المدارس الحكومية في نظام التعليم العام في المملكة العربية السعودية
The Institute of Art Education established its first institute in Riyadh, Saudi Arabia	**1965**	أســس معهــد التربيــة الفنيــة أول مركــز لــه فــي الريــاض، المملكة العربية السعودية
Jaha went to study at the Institute of Art Education in Riyadh, Saudi Arabia	**1972**	بدأ يوســف جاهــا رحلته الفنية من خلال دراســته في معهد التربيــة الفنية في الرياض
The Saudi Arabian Society for Culture and Arts was established in Riyadh, Saudi Arabia, which later opened thirteen branches accross Saudi Arabia. Jaha participated in many of their exhibitions starting 1983	**1973**	تأسســت الجمعية العربية الســعودية للثقافــة والفنون في الريــاض، فافتتحــت في الســنوات التالية 13 فرعًــا في جميع أنحــاء المملكة، وشــارك جاها في العديد مــن معارضها بدءًا من عــام 1983م
The General Presidency of Youth Welfare was established as an independent governmental institution with a dedicated department for fine arts	**1974**	تأسست الرئاسة العامة لرعاية الشباب كجهة حكومية مستقلة، تضم قسمًا متخصصًا في الفنون الجميلة، تقيم معارض سنوية تشمل معرض الفن السعودي المعاصر ومعرض مجموعة الفنون التشكيلية والمعرض العام لمناطق المملكة العربية السعودية
Mohammed Alsaleem founded The Saudi Art House in Riyadh, Saudi Arabia, where Jaha engaged with prominent artists in the local art community	**1979**	أســس محمــد الســليم دار الفنــون الســعودية فــي الريــاض، حيــث التقــى جاهــا بفنانيــن بارزيــن فــي المجتمــع الفني المحلي
Jaha received the first prize at *The Third General Art Exhibition* in Riyadh, Saudi Arabia, organized by The General Presidency of Youth Welfare, marking an early recognition of his talent		حصــل جاهــا علــى جائــزة المركــز الأول في (المعــرض الفني العــام في دورتــه الثالثة) فــي الرياض والذي نظمته الرئاســة العامة لرعاية الشباب
Jaha won the first prize at *The Fifth General Exhibition for the Regions of the Kingdom* by The General Presidency of Youth Welfare	**1982**	حصــل جاهــا علــى جائــزة المركــز الأول في (المعــرض الفني العــام في دورتــه الثالثة) فــي الرياض والذي نظمته الرئاســة العامة لرعاية الشباب
Jaha became an art teacher at Alfaisaliah School in Makkah, Saudi Arabia		أصبح معلّمًا للتربية الفنية فــي مدارس الفيصلية النموذجية في مكة المكرمة
Jaha obtained a Bachelor of Arts from Umm Al-Qura University in Makkah, Saudi Arabia	**1983**	حصل على شــهادة البكالوريــوس في الفنون مــن جامعة أم القرى في مكة المكرمة
Jaha participated in a group exhibition at The Golden Sail Gallery in Kuwait		شــارك مع مجموعة من الفنانين في معرض الشراع الذهبي في الكويت
Jaha participated in two international exhibitions, *The Arts and Culture of Saudi* exhibition in Italy, and Saudi Art Exhibition in Turkey	**1984**	شارك في معرضين دوليين «معرض الفنون والثقافة السعودية في إيطاليا» ومعرض «الفن السعودي في تركيا»
GCC Arts Friends Group was founded by artists Abdulrahman Alsoliman and Dr. Fouad Mougharbel. This initiative organized exhibitions across the world for artists from the GCC	**1985**	أســس الفنانــان عبدالرحمن الســليمان والدكتور فــؤاد مغربل «جماعة أصدقاء الفن التشكيلي» في الخليج، وقد نظمت هذه المبادرة معارض للفنانين الخليجيين في جميع أنحاء العالم
Jaha held his first solo exhibition at Rochan Gallery in Jeddah, Saudi Arabia. This was a significant milestone in his art career	**1987**	أقــام الفنــان يوســف جاهــا أول معرض فــردي له فــي صالة روشــان فــي جــدة والتي تأسســت فــي عــام 1980م

Jaha participated in the 19th International Awards for Contemporary Arts in France	**1987**	شـارك في الجائـزة الدولية التاسعة عشـرة للفنون المعاصرة في فرنسا
Jaha won the first prize of the 11th Formative Arts Collection exhibition by The General Presidency of Youth Welfare	**1988**	فاز بجائزة المركز الأول في معرض مجموعة الفنون التشكيلية الحادي عشر من تنظيم الرئاسة العامة لرعاية الشباب
Jaha received the Golden Palm Award during the first periodic for the Gulf Cooperation Council in Riyadh, Saudi Arabia	**1989**	حاز على جائزة النخلة الذهبية «Golden Palm» في الدورة الأولى لمجلس التعاون الخليجي في الرياض
Jaha participated in the 4th Asian Biennale in Bangladesh, nominated by General Presidency of Youth Welfare		شارك بترشـيح من الرئاسـة العامة لرعاية الشباب في معرض البينالي الآسيوي الرابع في بنغلادش
Al Muftaha Arts Village was founded in Abha, Saudi Arabia, by the Governor of Asir Prince Khalid bin Faisal AlSaud. Jaha participated in the group show at the opening ceremony		تأسسـت قرية المفتاحـة الفنية في أبها برئاسـة أمير منطقة عسـير، الأمير خالد بن فيصل آل سعود، حيث شارك يوسف جاها في معرضها الافتتاحي الجماعي
Jaha won the first prize at the *Islamic Heritage* exhibition in Riyadh, Saudi Arabia	**1990**	فـاز بالمركـز الأول في معرض التراث الإسـلامي فـي الرياض، المملكة العربية السعودية
Jaha won the first prize in the first Malwan Art Competition by the Saudi Arabian Airlines	**1992**	فاز فـي مسـابقة مَلون السـعودية التـي نظمتهـا الخطـوط الجوية السـعودية
Jaha participated in the Arab Islamic Contemporary Art exhibition in Turkey, nominated by Saudi Arabian Society for Culture and Arts	**1993**	شـارك فـي معـرض الفـن العربـي الإسـلامي المعاصـر فـي تركيـا، بترشـيح مـن الجمعيـة العربية السـعودية للثقافة والفنون
The House of Artists was founded in Jeddah, Saudi Arabia. Jaha participated in their exhibitions		شـارك في معـرض بيت التشـكيليين الذي تأسـس في جدة، المملكة العربية السعودية في العام نفسـه
Jaha received Al-Danah Award for the *25th of February* art exhibition in Kuwait. Jaha won first prize at Malwan Art Competition by the Saudi Arabian Airlines for the second time	**1997**	حصل على جائزة الدانة في معرض الفن الخامس والعشرين من فبراير في الكويت، كما فاز للمرة الثانية في مسابقة مَلون للفنون التي نظمتها الخطوط الجوية السعودية
Jaha was nominated by The General Presidency of Youth Welfare to exhibit at the eighth *Cairo International Biennale* in Cairo, Egypt	**2001**	رشـحته الرئاسـة العامة لرعاية الشـباب للمشاركة في بينالي القاهـرة الدولـي الثامن فـي القاهرة، مصر
Makkah Group for Fine Arts was established by a group of artists including Jaha, led by artist Hasan Abdulmajeed	**2003**	أسسـت مجموعة من الفنانين، ومن ضمنهم يوسـف جاها، مجموعـة مكة للفنون الجميلة، وكان يقودها الفنان حسـن عبدالمجيد
Jaha held his fourth solo exhibition at Al-Alalamiah Gallery in Jeddah, Saudi Arabia	**2005**	أقـام الفنان يوسـف جاها معرضه الفردي الرابع في معرض العالميـة في جدة
Jaha became a full-time artist	**2008**	تفرغ الفنان يوسف جاها للفن تفرغاً كاملاً
Jaha participated in Contemporary Art from Saudi Arabia, organized by Edge of Arabia in London, the United Kingdom. His work was acquired by Aramco		شارك في معرض «Contemporary Art from Saudi Arabia» بتنسيق من «Edge of Arabia» في لندن، كما اقتنى أعماله مجموعة من الأفراد والمؤسسات منها «أرامكو»
Jaha received the Beautifying Holy Makkah Prize	**2010**	حصل على جائزة تجميل مكة المكرمة
Jaha participated in *Pulse 2* exhibition with artist Ahmed Felemban at Hafez Gallery in Jeddah, Saudi Arabia	**2017**	شـارك جاها في معرض «نبض 2» مع الفنـان أحمد فلمبان في حافظ غاليري في جدة، المملكة العربية السعودية
Misk Art Institute was established in Riyadh, Saudi Arabia		تأسس معهد مسك للفنون في الرياض، المملكة العربية السعودية
Jaha was honored by Misk Art Institute as a pioneer in the Saudi Arts	**2018**	حصل يوسـف جاها على جائزة كأحد رواد الفن في المملكة العربية السـعودية، من معهد مسك للفنون
Jaha held his most recent solo exhibition at Mono Gallery in Riyadh, Saudi Arabia	**2019**	أقـام آخـر معارضه الفرديـة فـي مونو غاليـري فـي الرياض، المملكة العربية السعودية
Jaha participated in *Echoing the Land* group exhibition featuring Saudi pioneering artists, by Misk Art Institute in Riyadh, Saudi Arabia	**2023**	شـارك في معرض «من حولهـم» لمجموعة مـن رواد الفن السـعودي، مـن تنظيم معهـد مسـك للفنون فـي الرياض، المملكـة العربية السـعودية

الأعمـــال
الفنيــة
Artworks

*Makkah Wooden Windows
(Rawasheen)*, 1991

Oil on canvas
63 × 77 cm
Courtesy of the artist

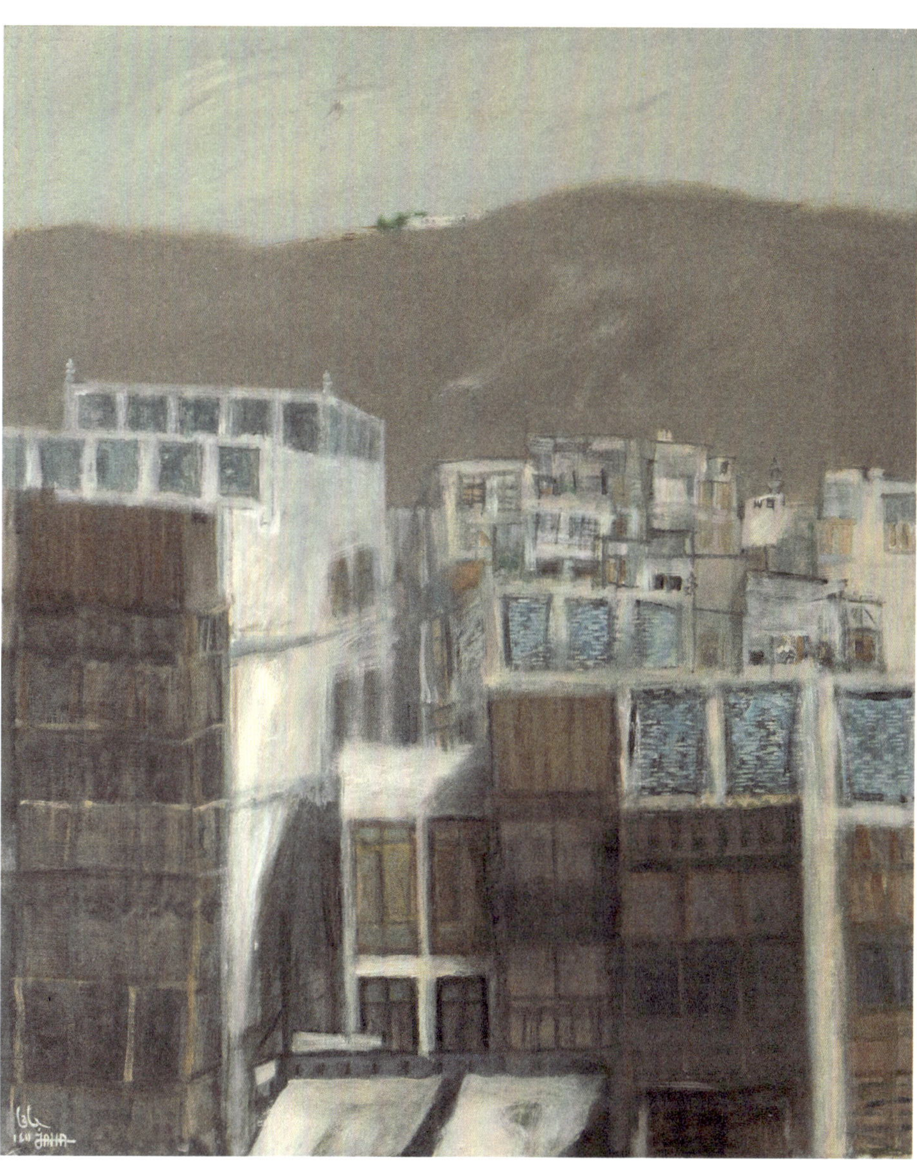

Untitled, 1998

Oil on canvas
90 × 100 cm
Courtesy of Mono Gallery

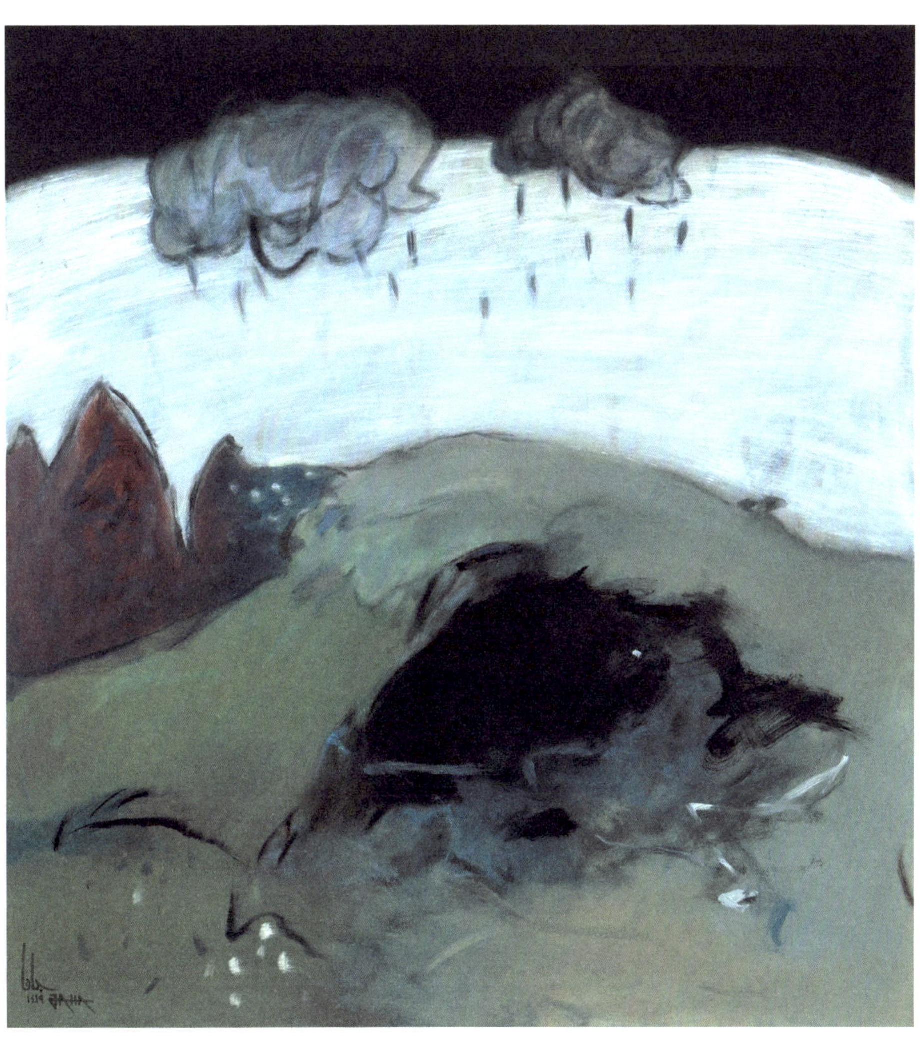

Untitled, 2000

Oil on canvas
145 × 145 cm
Courtesy of Al-Mansouria Foundation

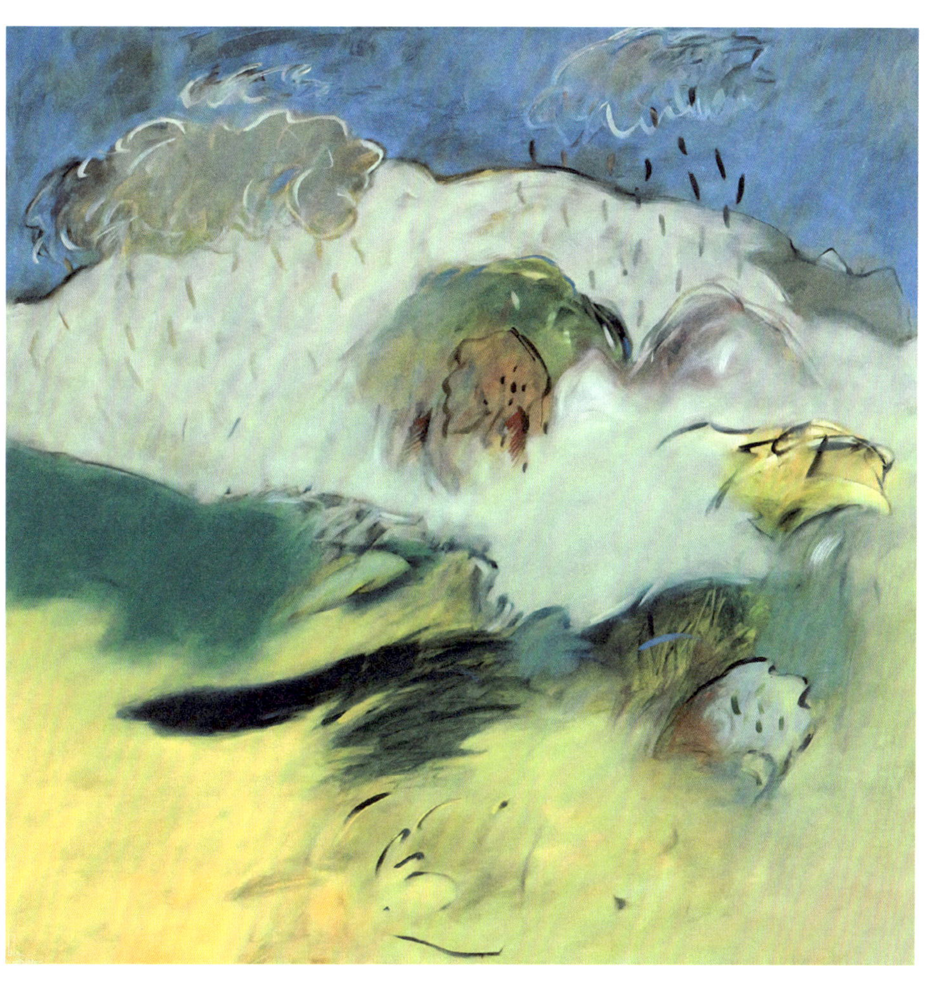

بدون عنوان، 2000م

ألوان أكريليك على ورق
30 × 30 سم
بإذن من مؤسسة المنصورية

Untitled, 2000

Acrylic on paper
30 × 30 cm
Courtesy of Al-Mansouria Foundation

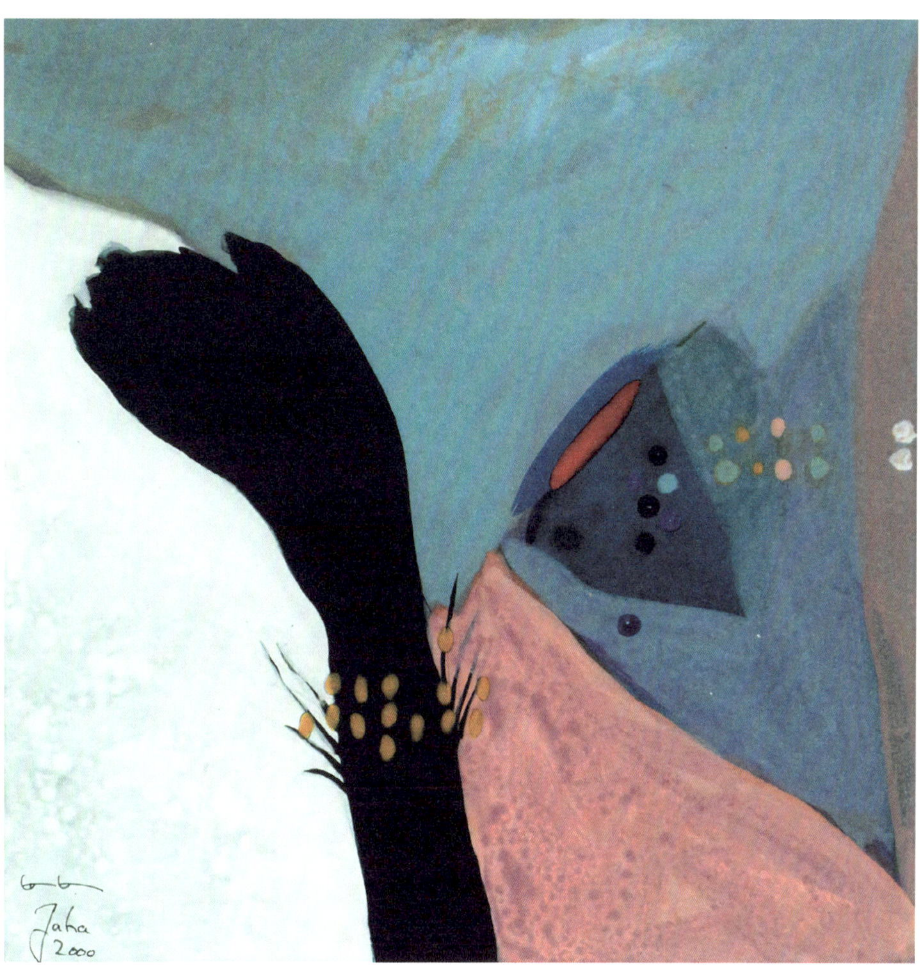
Jaha
2000

بدون عنوان، 2004م

ألوان زيتية على قماش
90 × 100 سم
بإذن من مونو غاليري

Untitled, 2004

Oil on canvas
90 × 100 cm
Courtesy of Mono Gallery

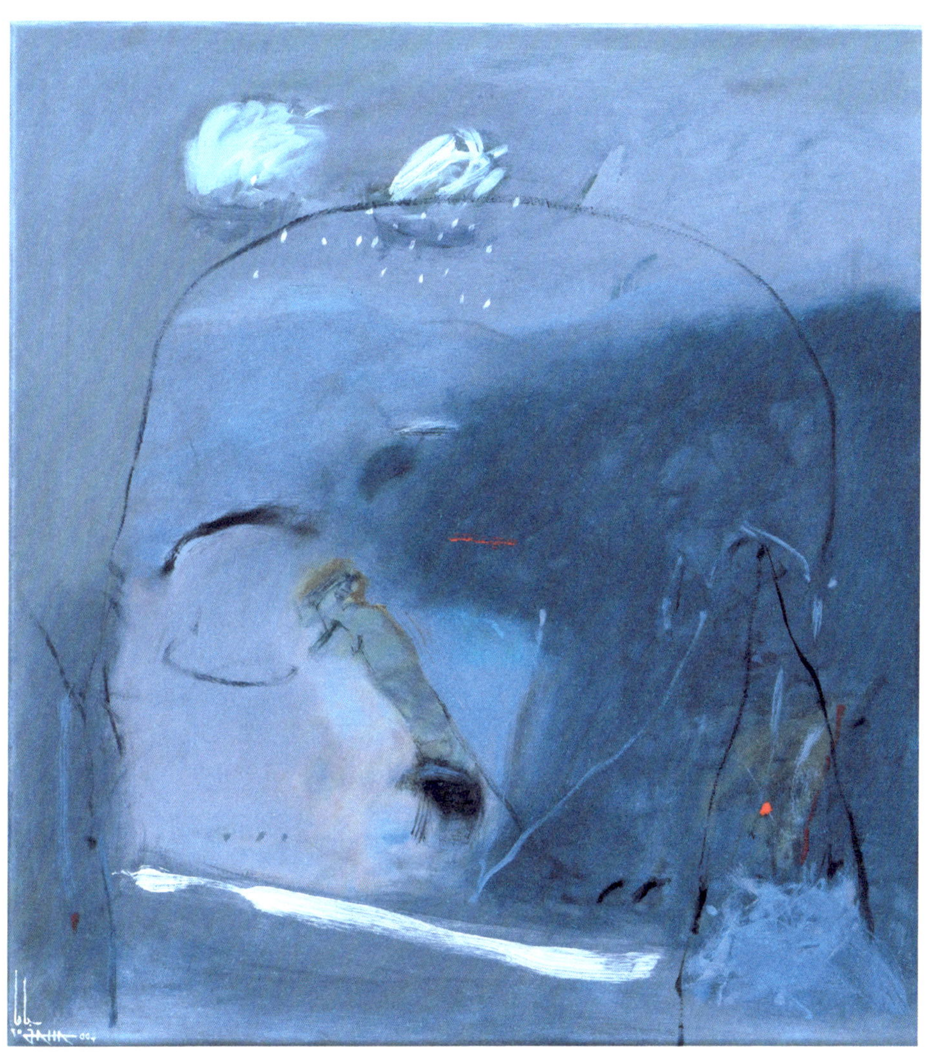

نبض الطبيعة، 2004م

ألوان زيتية على قماش
99 × 92 سم
بإذن من الفنان

The Nature's Beat, 2004

Oil on canvas
99 × 92 cm
Courtesy of the artist

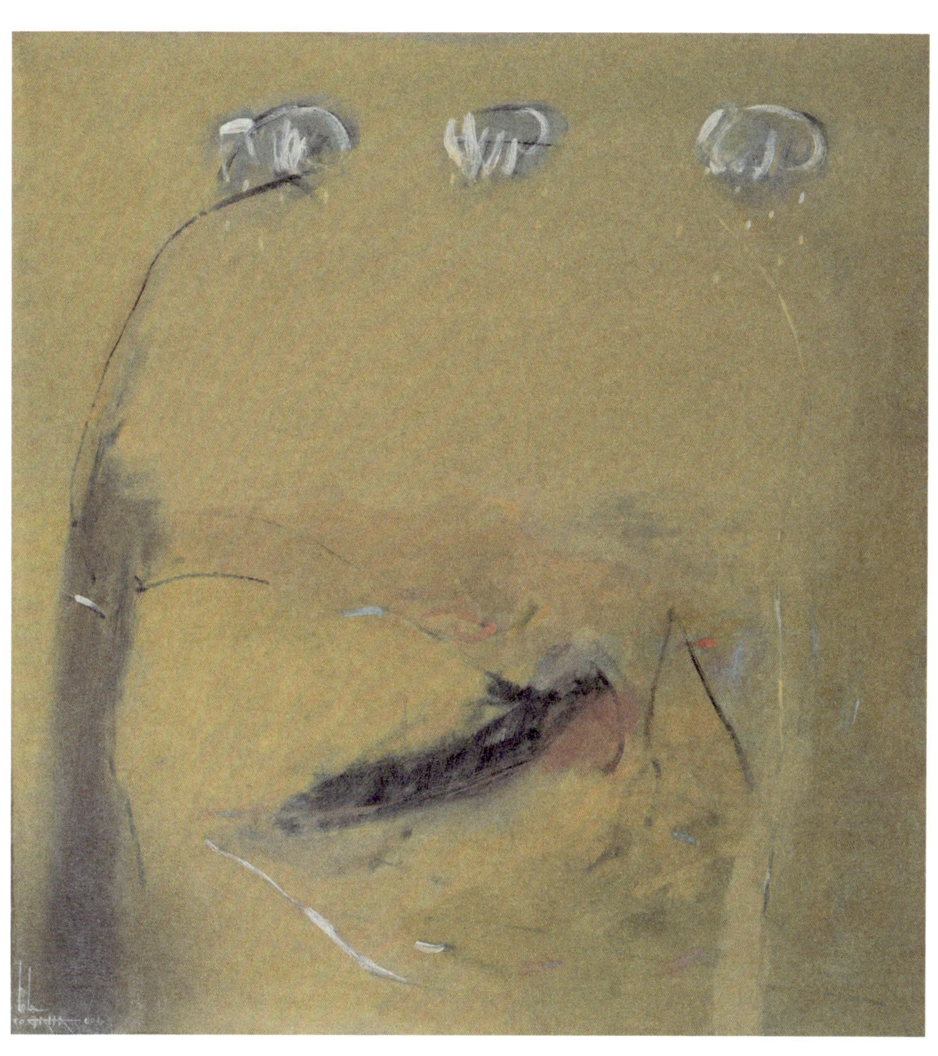

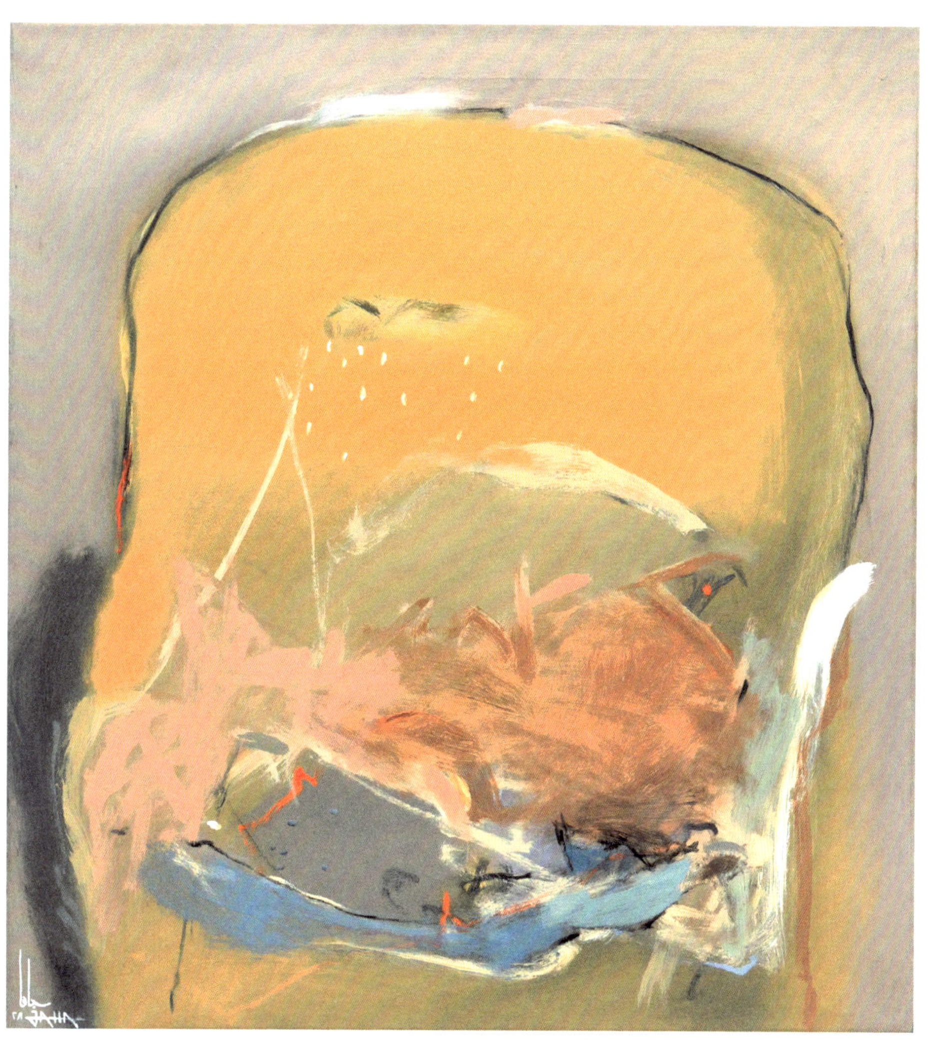

بدون عنوان، 2009م

ألوان أكريليك على ورق
30 × 30 سم
مجموعة خاصة

Untitled, 2009

Acrylic on paper
30 × 30 cm
Private collection

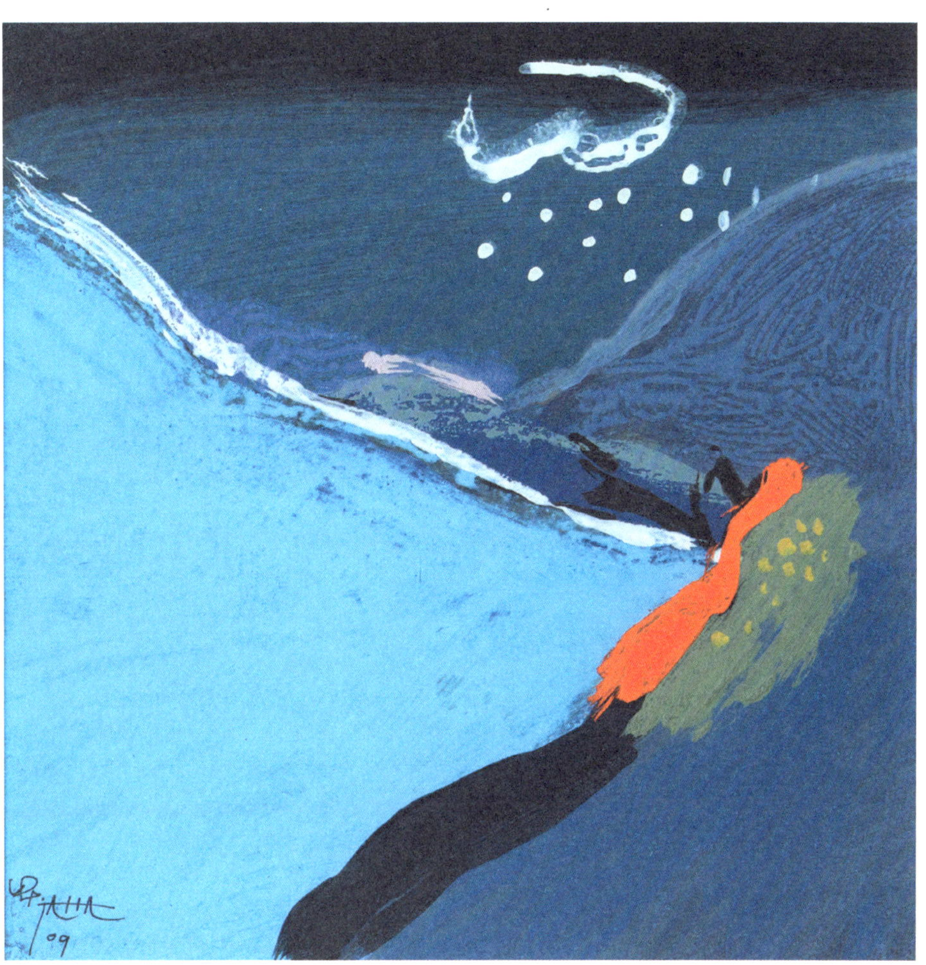

بدون عنوان، 2010م

ألوان أكريليك على ورق
30 × 30 سم
مجموعة خاصة

Untitled, 2010

Acrylic on paper
30 × 30 cm
Private collection

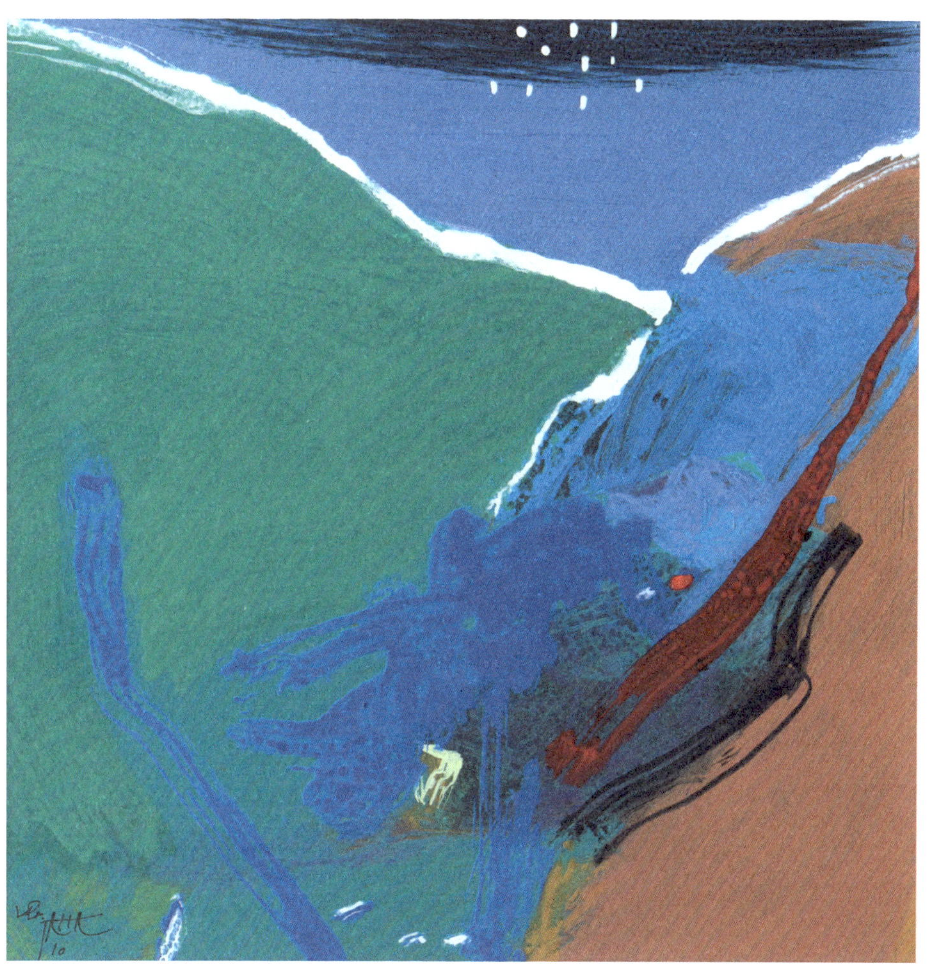

مباني الأحياء الشعبية
في مكة المكرمة، 2010م

ألوان زيتية على قماش
71 × 56 سم
بإذن من الفنان

*Buildings of Old Makkah
Neighborhoods*, 2010

Oil on canvas
71 × 56 cm
Courtesy of the artist

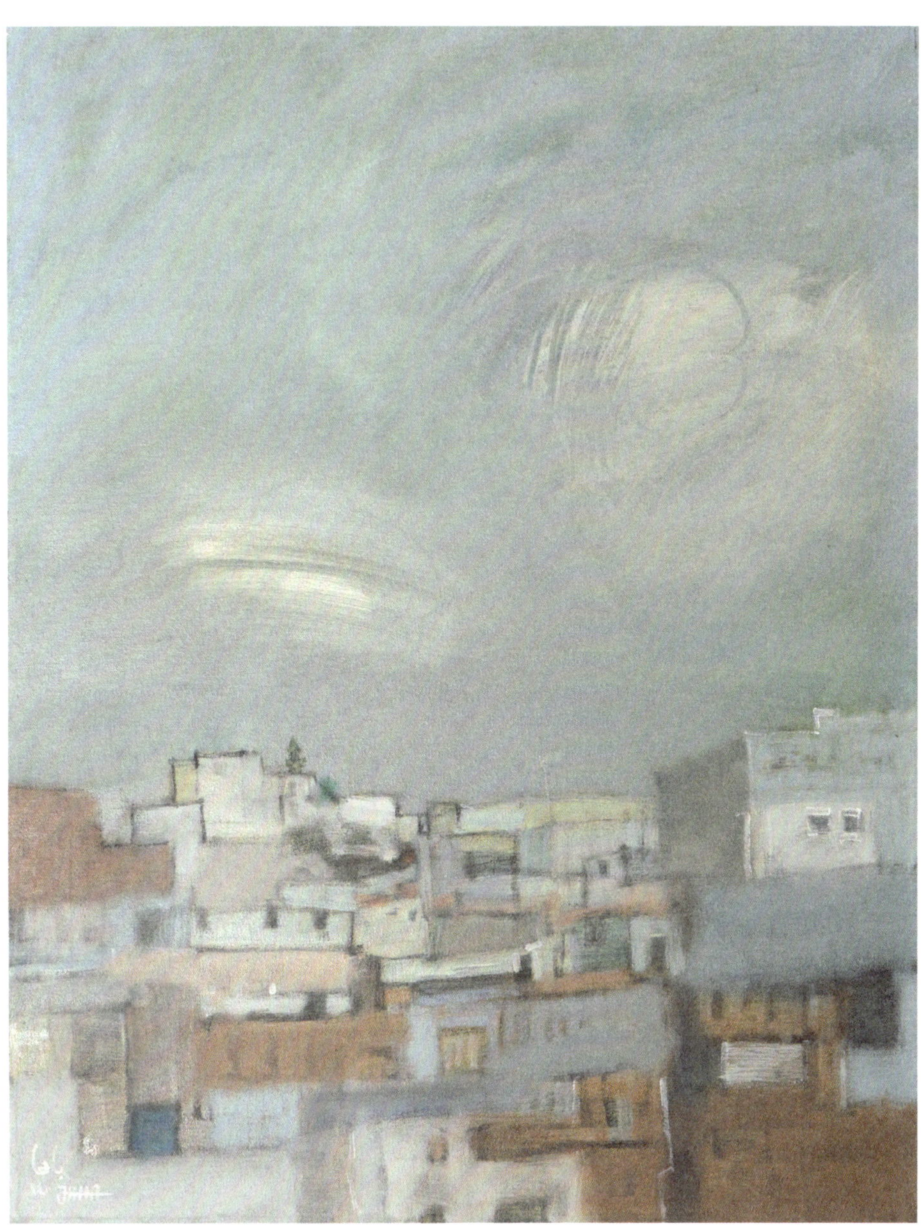

نبض الطبيعة، 2010م

The Nature's Beat, 2010

Acrylic on paper
30 × 30 cm
Courtesy of the artist

ألوان أكريليك على ورق
30 × 30 سم
بإذن من الفنان

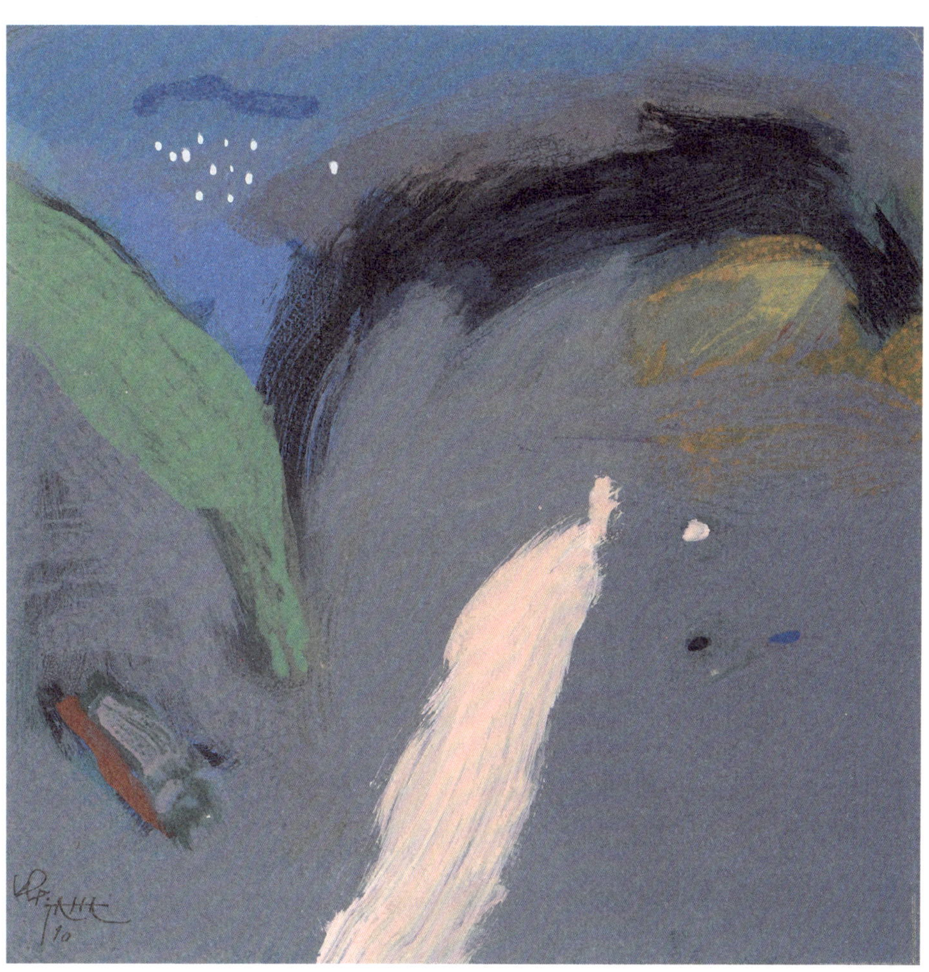

بدون عنوان، 2011م

ألوان زيتية على قماش
150 × 150 سم
بإذن من حافظ غاليري

Untitled, 2011

Oil on canvas
150 × 150 cm
Courtesy of Hafez Gallery

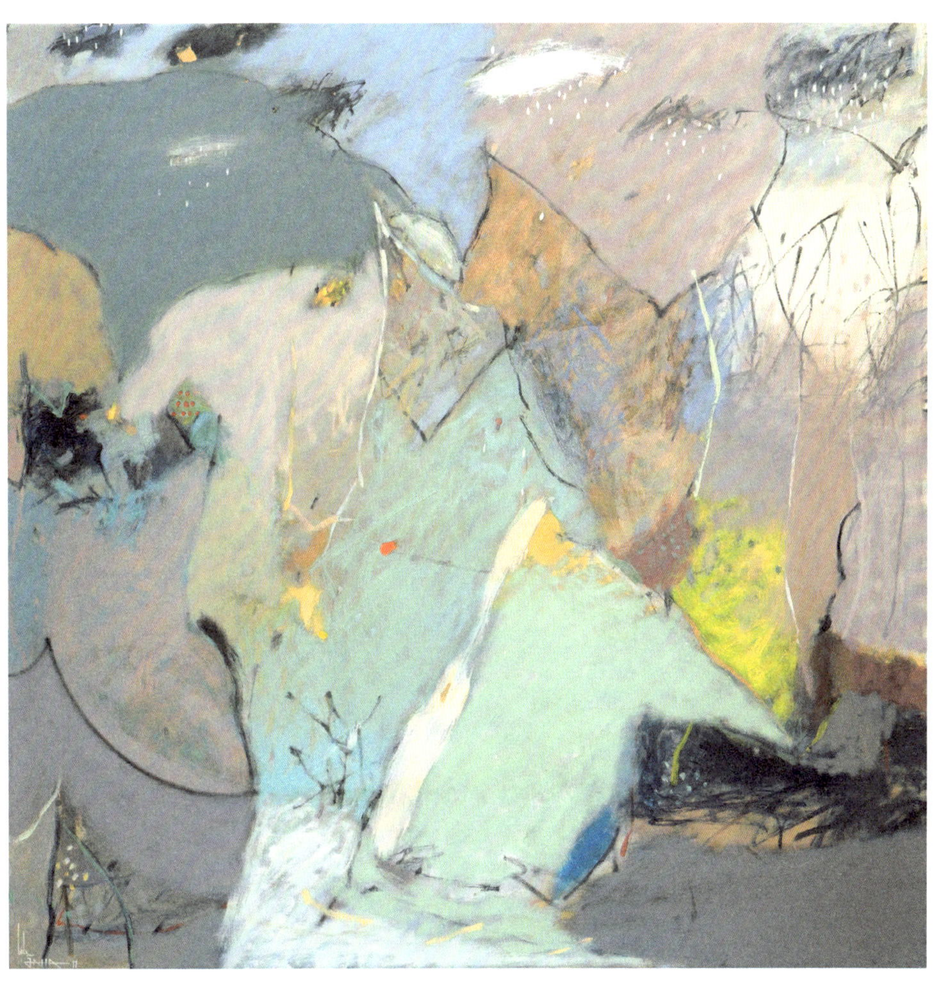

Untitled, 2012

Oil on canvas
150 × 150 cm
Courtesy of Hafez Gallery

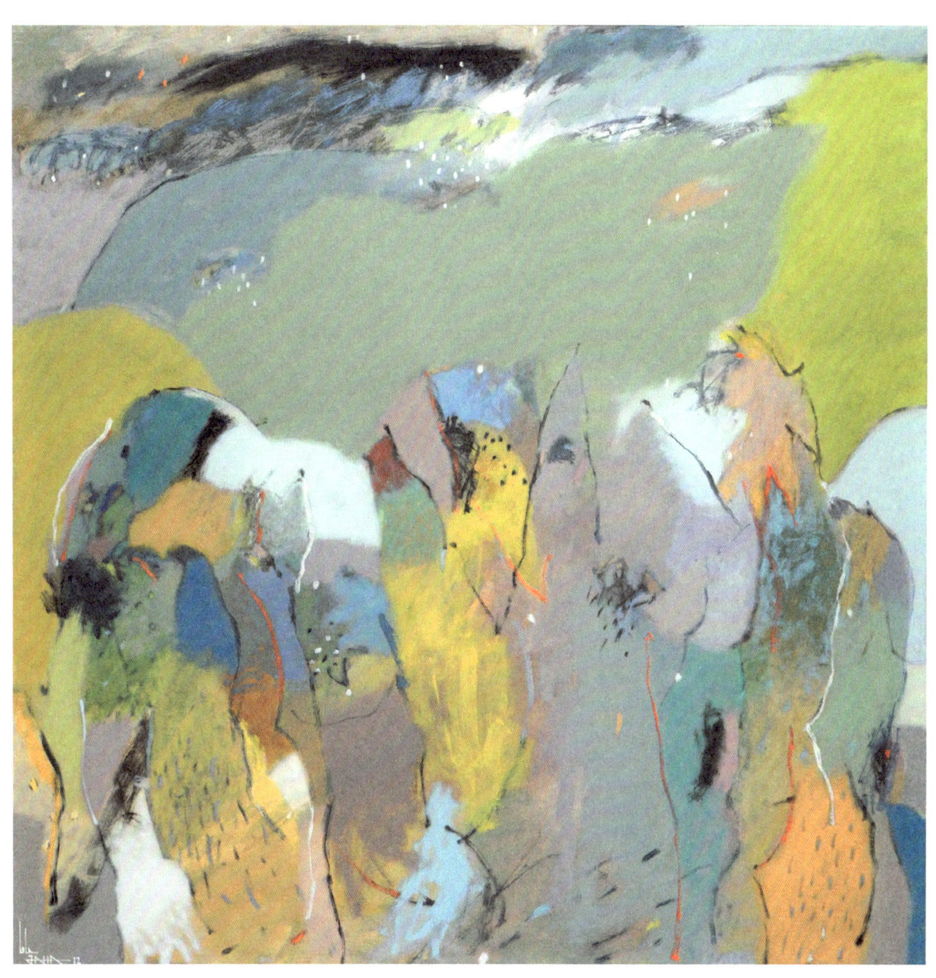

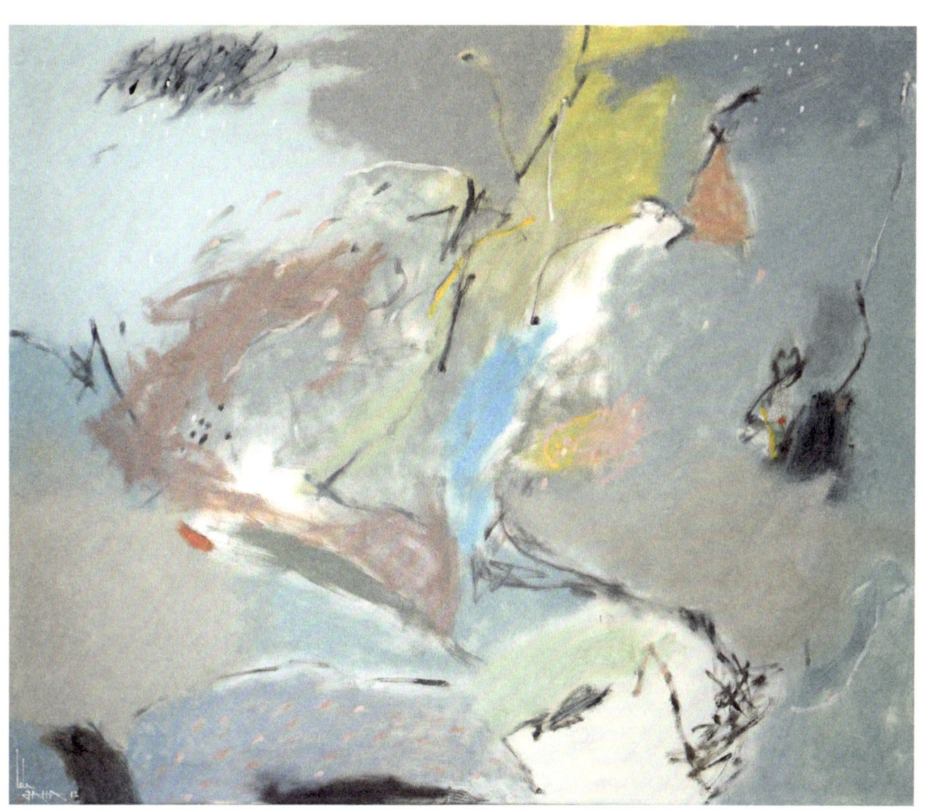

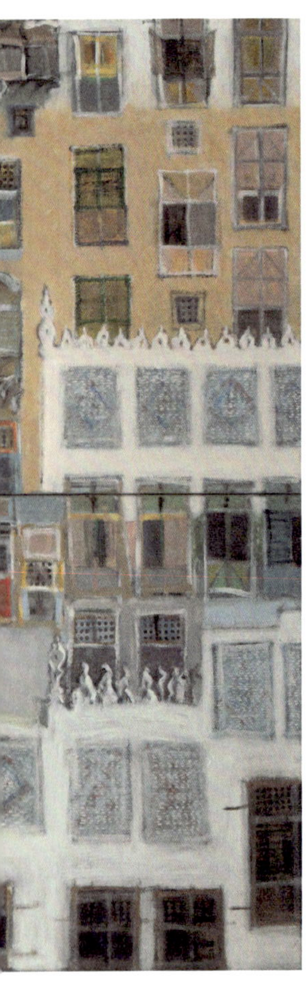

Makkah Buildings, 2013

Oil on canvas
120 × 190 cm
Courtesy of the artist

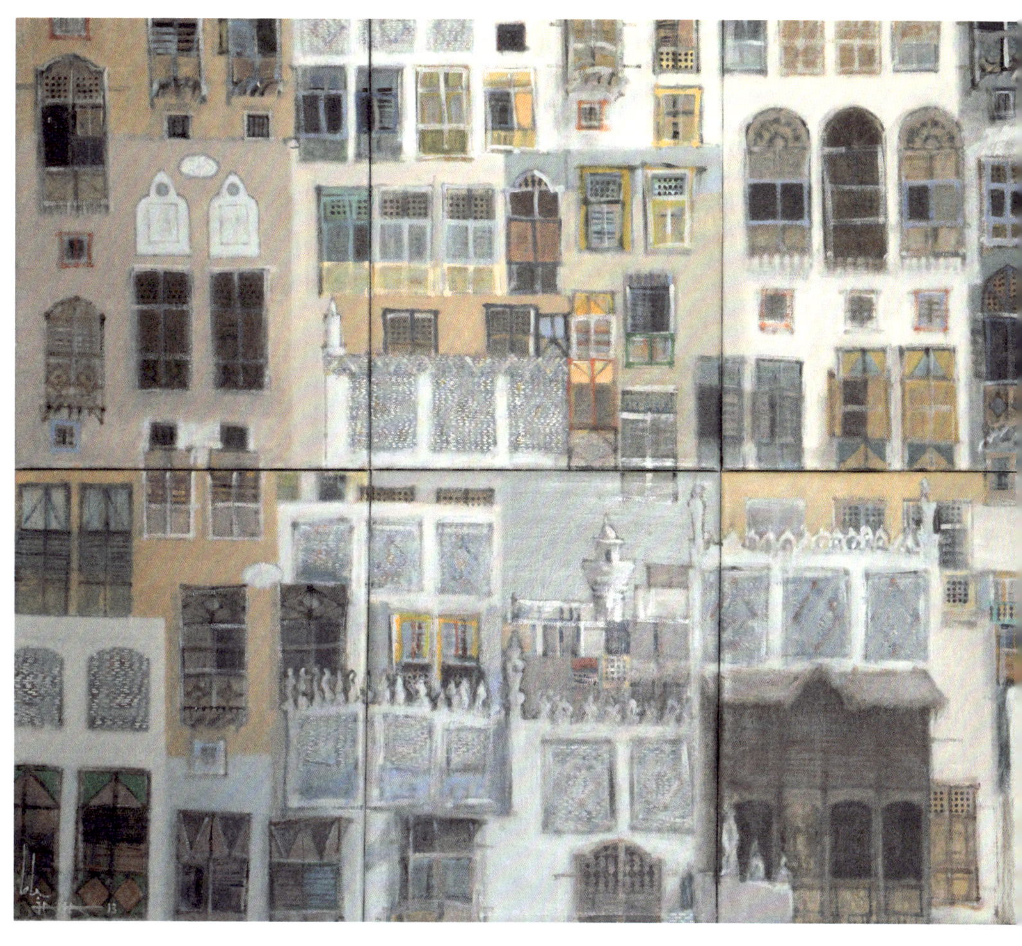

Untitled, 2013

بدون عنوان، 2013م

ألوان زيتية على قماش
105 × 125 سم
بإذن من مونو غاليري

Oil on canvas
105 × 125 cm
Courtesy of Mono Gallery

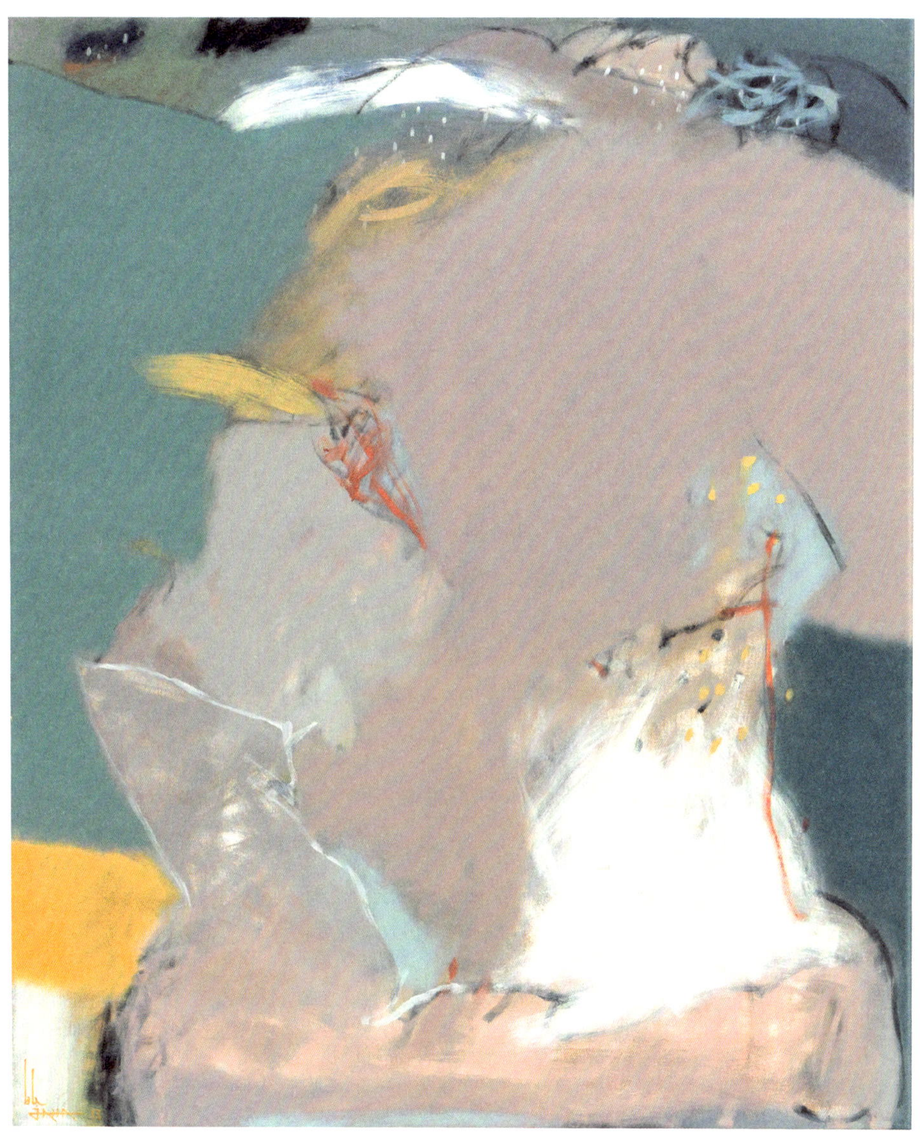

Untitled, 2014

Oil on canvas
125 × 125 cm
Courtesy of Mono Gallery

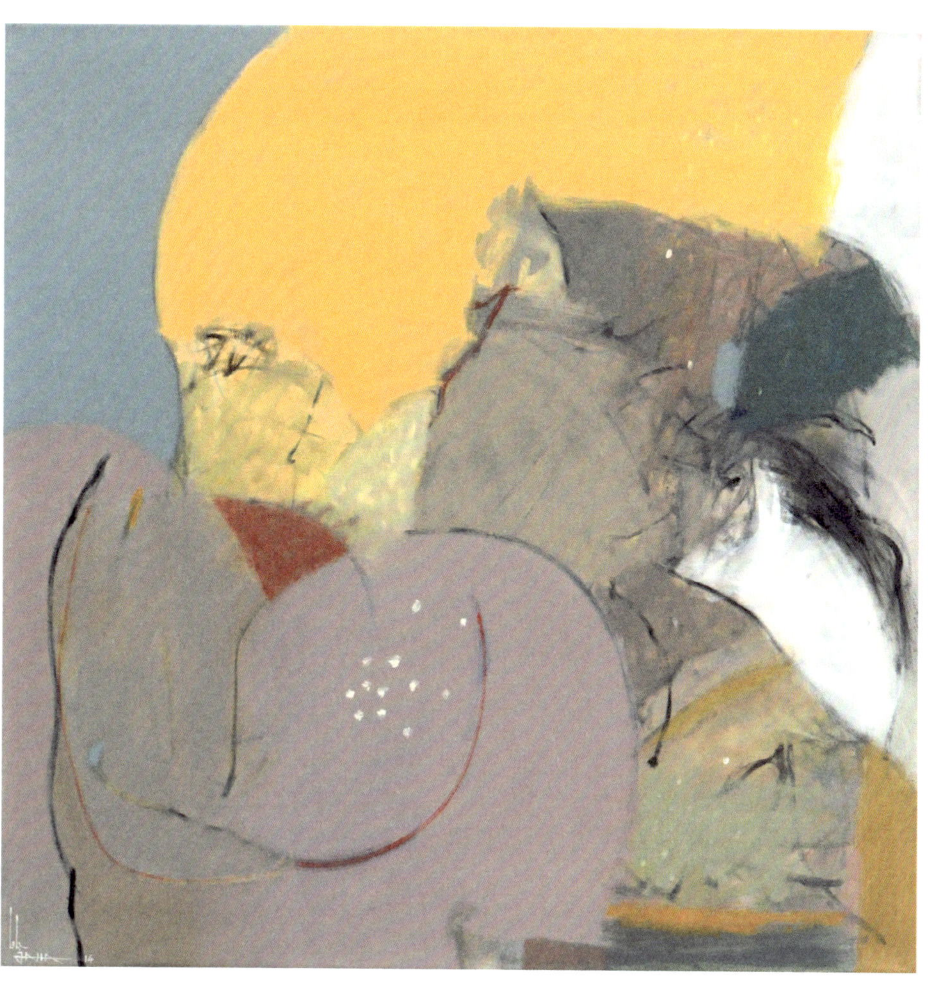

نبض الطبيعة، 2015م

ألوان زيتية على قماش
92 × 99 سم
بإذن من الفنان

The Nature's Beat, 2015

Oil on canvas
92 × 99 cm
Courtesy of the artist

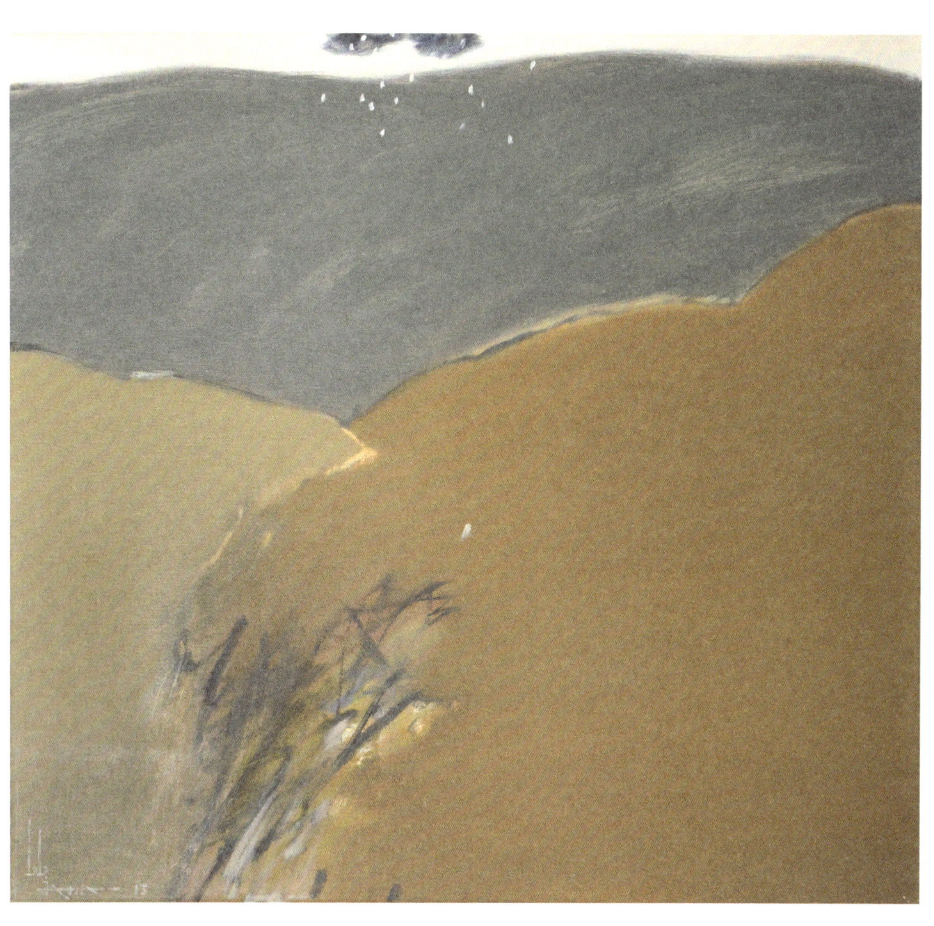

بدون عنوان، 2015م

ألوان زيتية على قماش
100 × 100 سم
بإذن من مونو غاليري

Untitled, 2015

Oil on canvas
100 × 100 cm
Courtesy of Mono Gallery

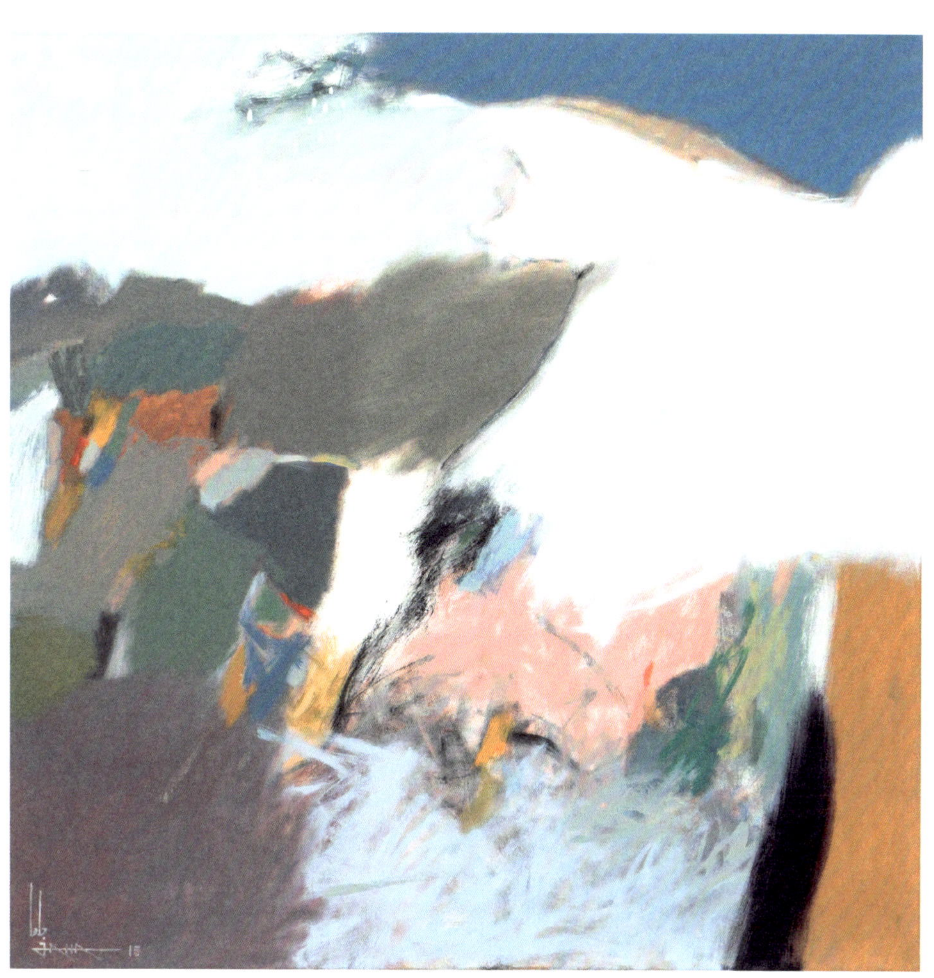

Untitled, 2015

Oil on canvas
49 × 49 cm
Courtesy of Hamza Serafi

بدون عنوان، 2015م

ألوان زيتية على قماش
49 × 49 سم
بإذن من حمزة صيرفي

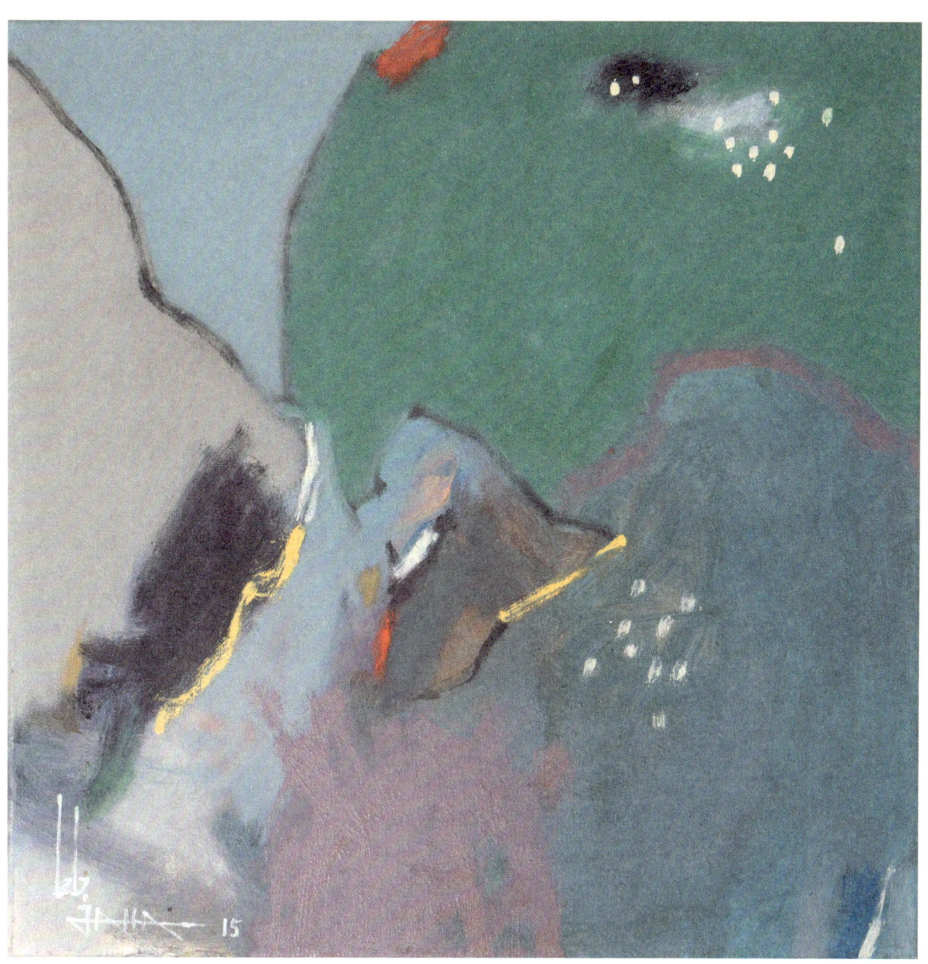

Untitled, 2017

Oil on canvas
125 × 125 cm
Courtesy of Mono Gallery

بدون عنوان، 2017م

ألوان زيتية على قماش
125 × 125 سم
بإذن من مونو غاليري

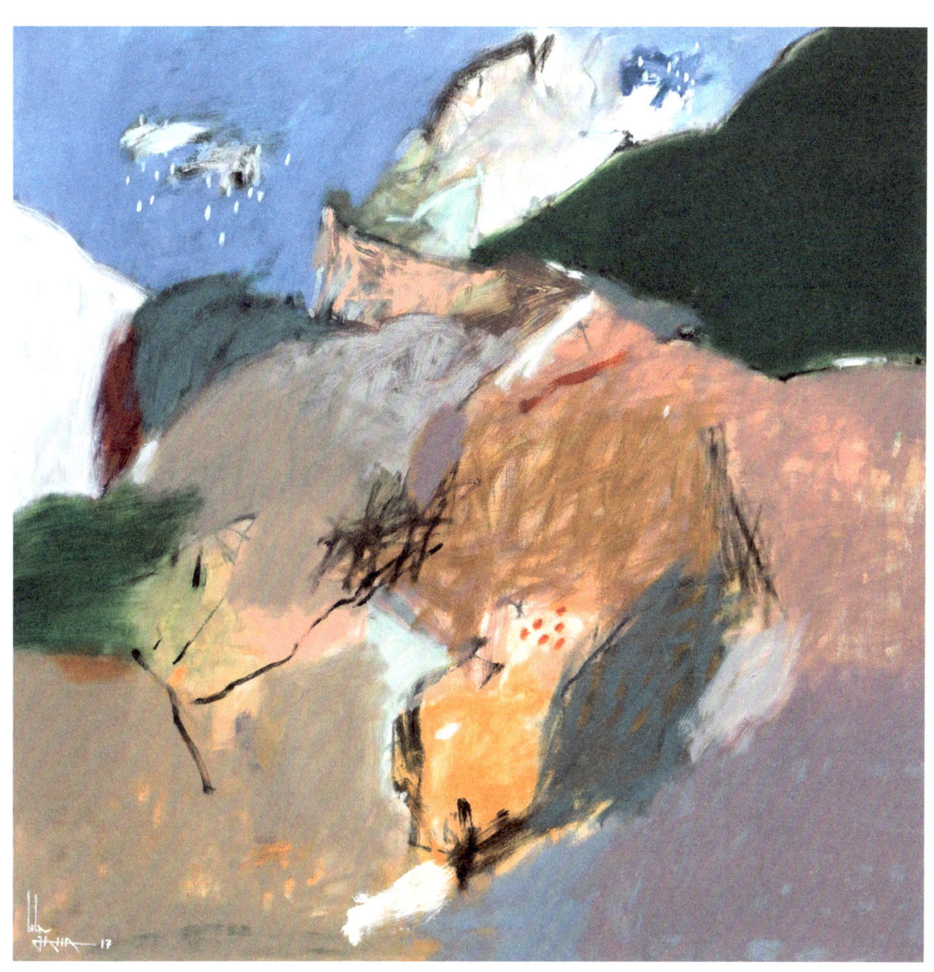

بدون عنوان، 2018م

ألوان زيتية على قماش

150 × 150 سم

بإذن من مونو غاليري

Untitled, 2018

Oil on canvas
150 × 150 cm
Courtesy of Mono Gallery

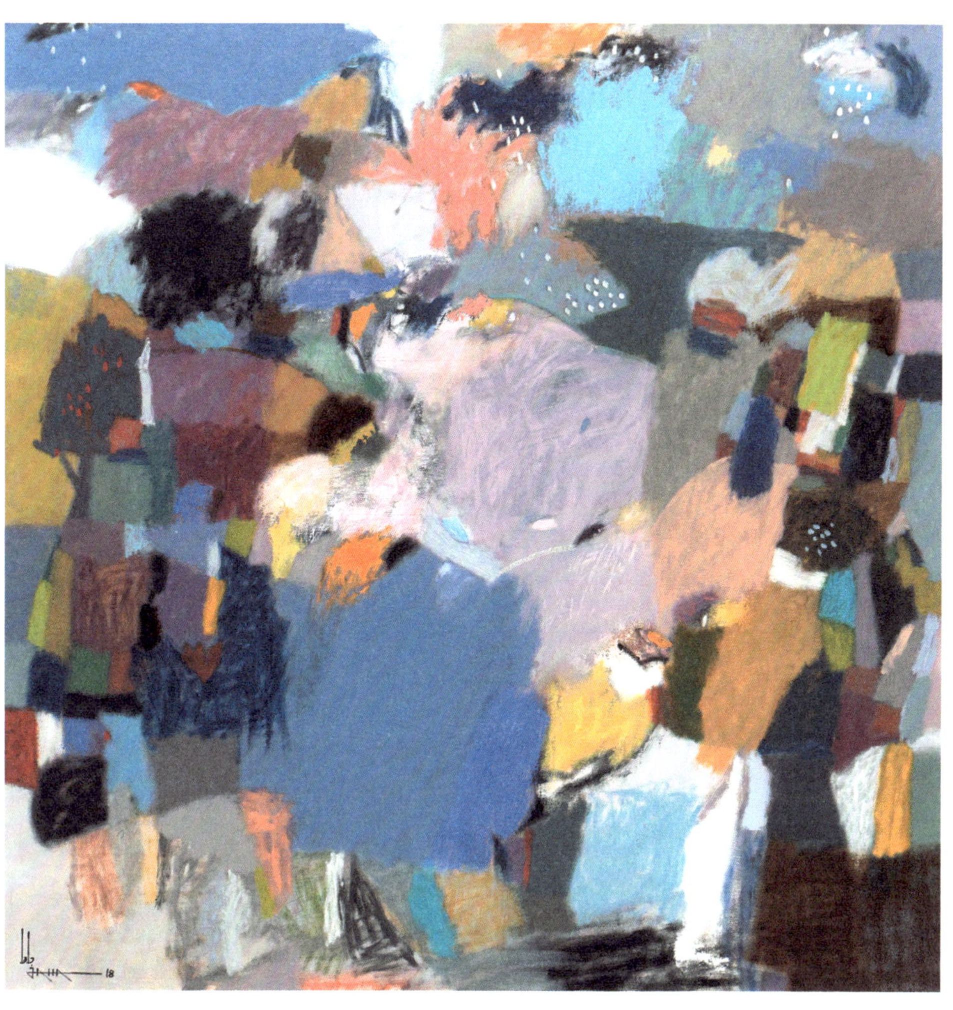

بدون عنوان، 2021م

ألوان زيتية على قماش
80 × 65 سم
بإذن من مونو غاليري

Untitled, 2021

Oil on canvas
80 × 65 cm
Courtesy of Mono Gallery

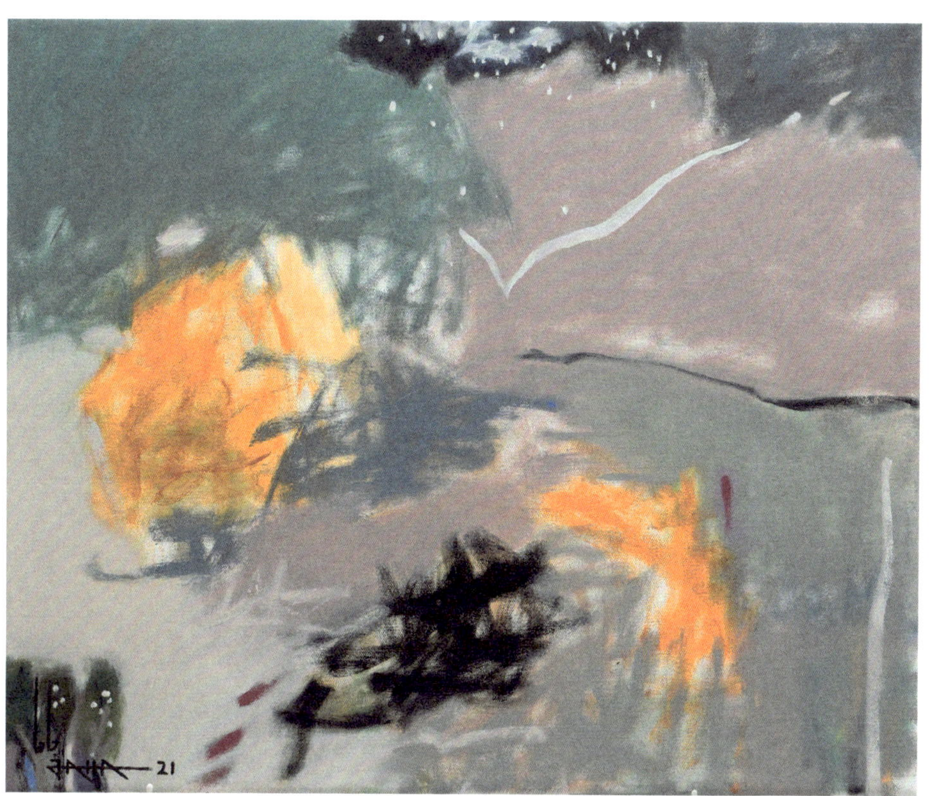

The Nature's Beat, 2022

Acrylic on paper
30 × 40 cm
Courtesy of the artist

ألوان أكريليك على ورق
30 × 40 سم
بإذن من الفنان

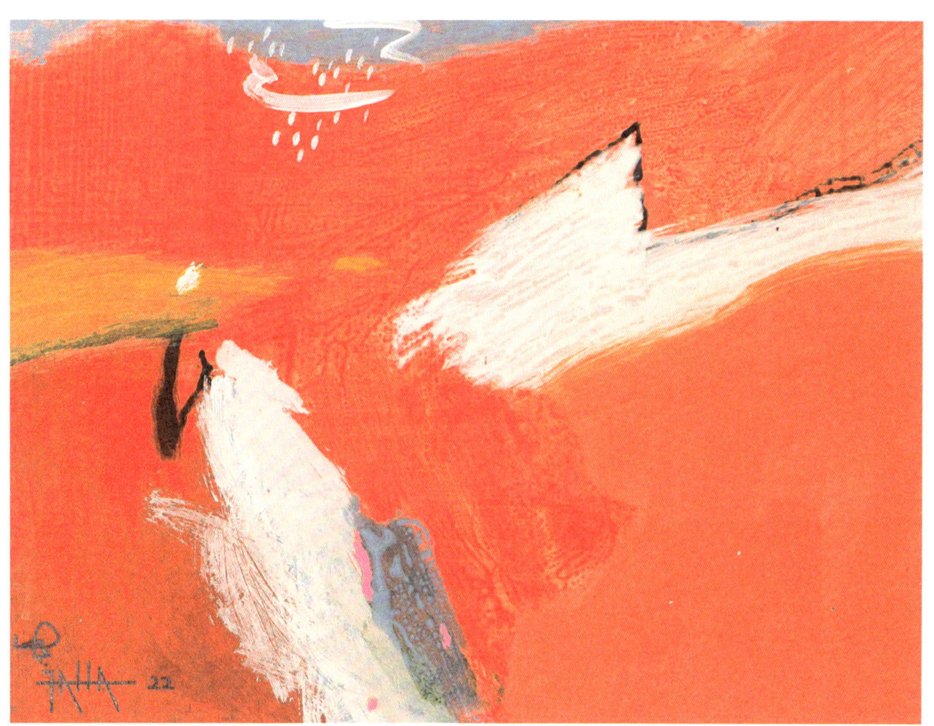

The Nature's Beat, 2022

Acrylic on paper
30 × 30 cm
Courtesy of the artist

نبض الطبيعة، 2022م

ألوان أكريليك على ورق
30 × 30 سم
بإذن من الفنان

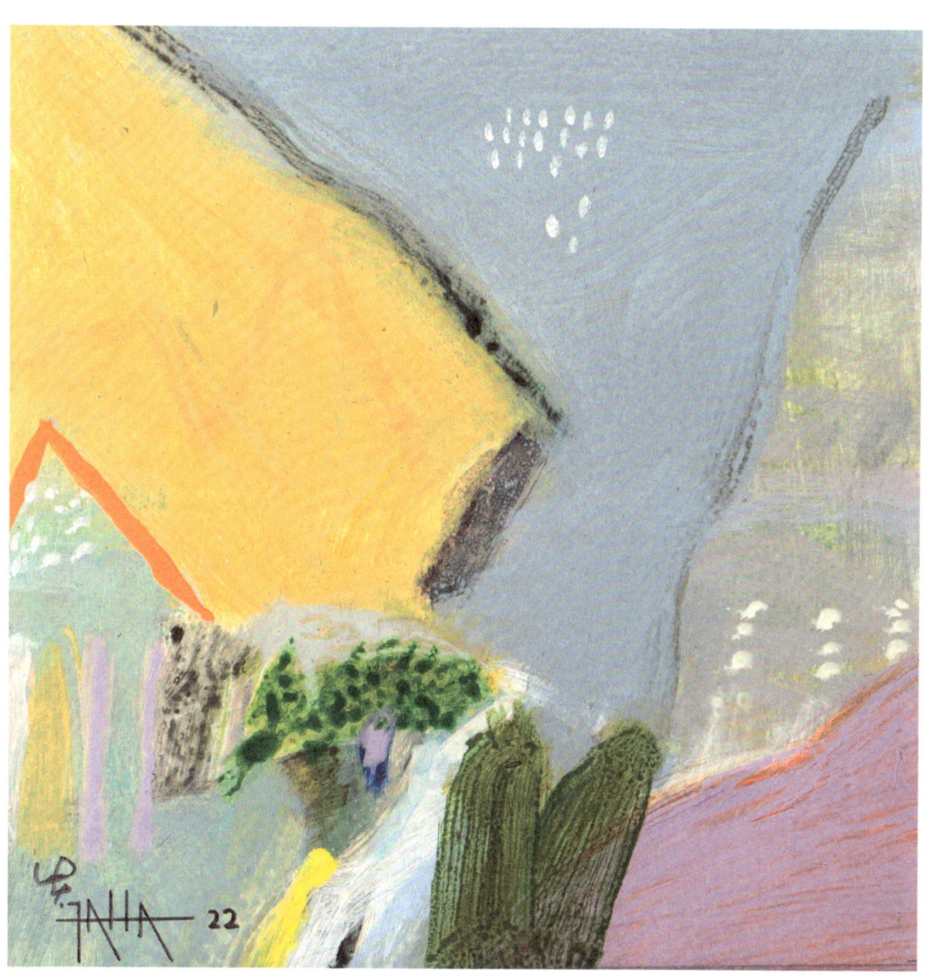

The Nature's Beat, 2022

Acrylic on paper
30 × 30 cm
Courtesy of the artist

نبض الطبيعة، 2022م

ألوان أكريليك على ورق
30 × 30 سم
بإذن من الفنان

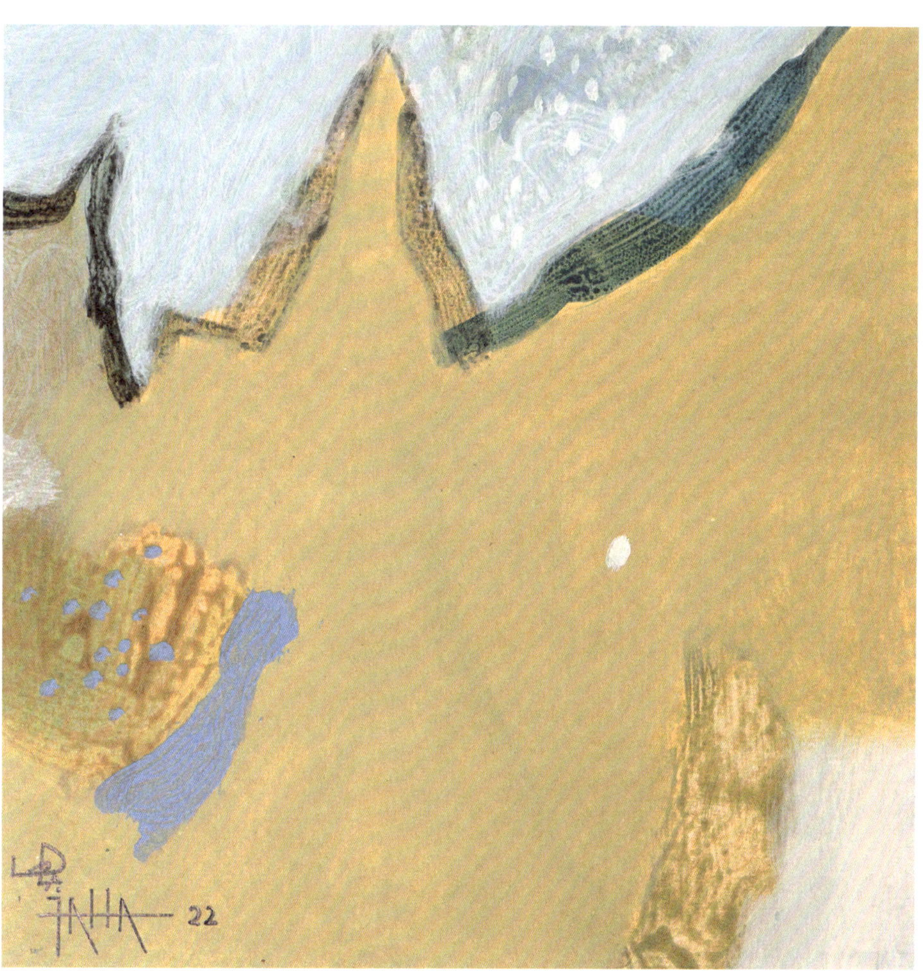

نبض الطبيعة، 2022م

ألوان أكريليك على ورق
30 × 40 سم
بإذن من الفنان

The Nature's Beat, 2022

Acrylic on paper
30 × 40 cm
Courtesy of the artist

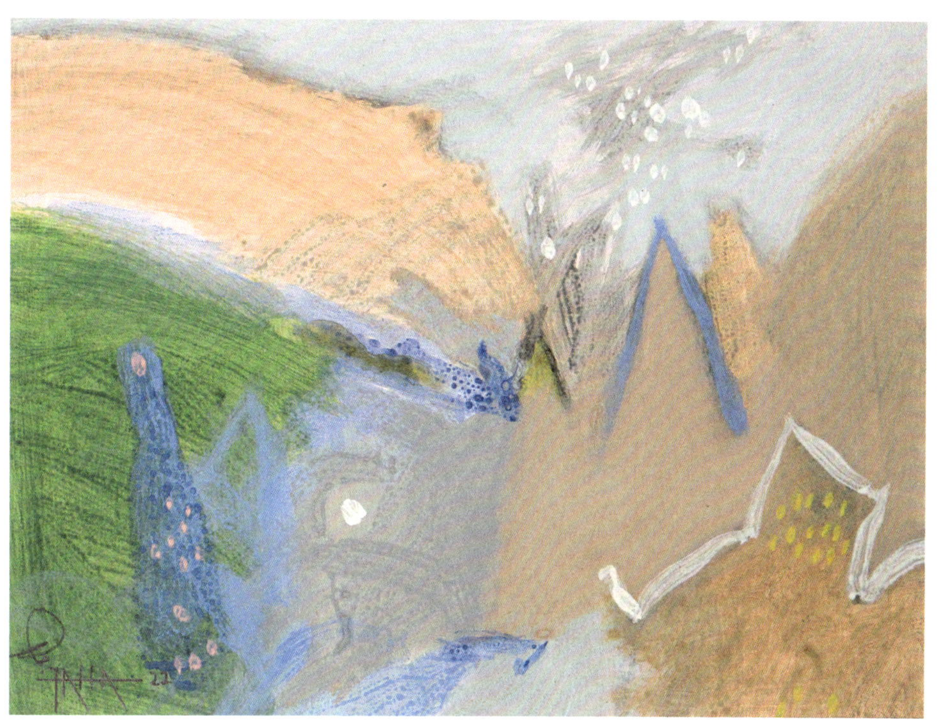

The Nature's Beat, 2022

Acrylic on paper
40 × 30 cm
Courtesy of the artist

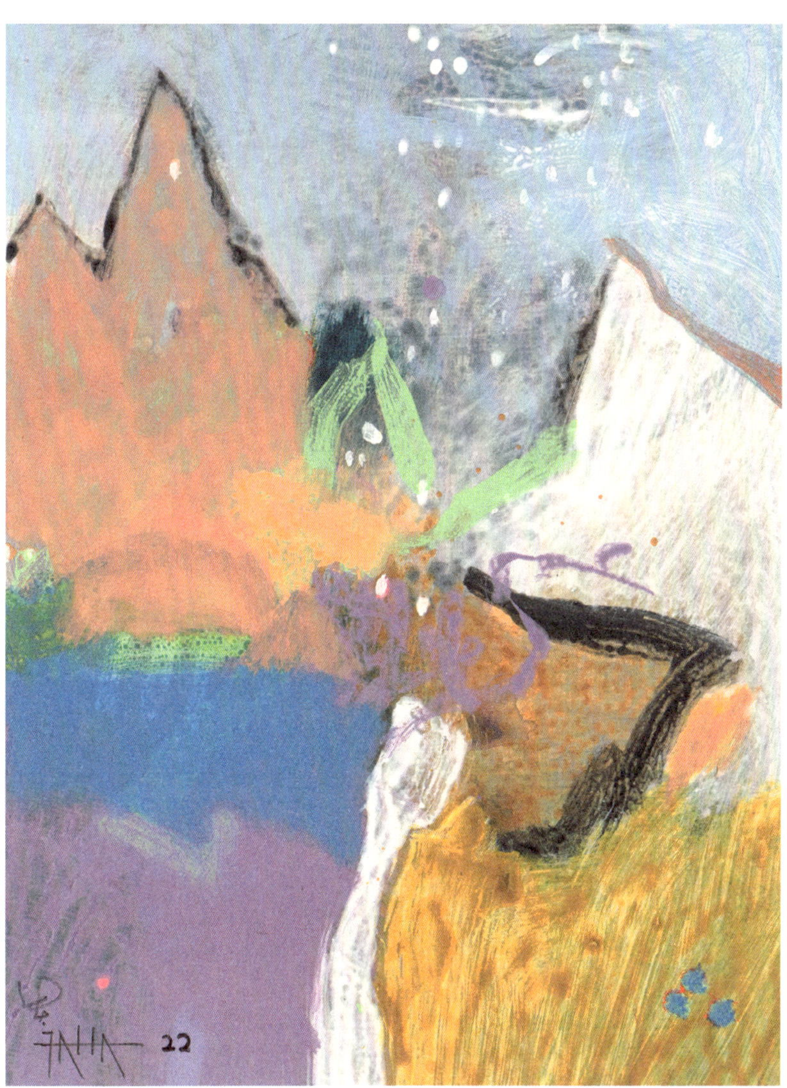

الفنان يوسفـــ أحمد جاها
The Artist
Yousef Ahmad Jaha

دكتور محمد فلفلان، عضو هيئة تدريس بجامعة أم القرى، باحث في الفنون البصرية
Dr. Mohammad Filfilan, Faculty member at Umm Al-Qura University, Visual Arts Researcher

The first generation of Saudi artists distinguished themselves with a visual richness that rivaled international contemporaries—a remarkable feat given the limited means of communication in a time predating modern technology. Many Saudi artists emerged from the 1970s through the 1990s embracing modern art methods and techniques while confronting the challenges of a scarcity of resources and society's acceptance of this kind of art. The Saudi government's support catalyzed the emergence of many artists during that period. Foreign scholarship programs, local competitions, exhibitions, and opportunities for international participation nurtured the professional growth and artistic practice of those who are now considered pioneering artists.

Yousef Ahmad Jaha from Makkah emerged as one of those pioneering artists who capitalized on the government's support, garnering numerous awards through local and international exhibitions. In the 1970s and 1980s, with a dearth of galleries, exhibitions, and specialized stores selling professional art tools in his city, Jaha made use of the limited resources available and honed his skills by practicing and educating himself visually and intellectually.

تميـز الرعيـل الأول مـن فنانـي المملكـة العربيـة السـعودية بثراء بصـري يضاهي الفنانيـن العالميـن؛ على الرغم من قلة المصادر والمعلومات في زمن لم تظهر فيه وسائل الاتصال الحديثة بعد. وبرز العديد من الفنانين السـعوديين في الفترة من السبعينيات إلى التسعينيات من القرن الماضي؛ بممارسة أساليب الفن الحديث وتقنياته المعاصرة، مواجهين تحديات نُدرة المصادر، وجدليّة تَقبُّل المجتمع لممارسة الفن واحترافِه. وقد أثمر اهتمـام حكومة المملكة العربية السـعودية في ظهـور العديد مـن الفنانين في تلك الفتـرة، وذلك مـن خلال برامـج الابتعـاث الخارجي وتفعيـل المسـابقات والمعـارض المحليـة، بالإضافة إلـى إتاحة الفرصة للفنانين بالمشـاركة في المحافل والمعـارض الدوليـة، ما سـاهم في تأصيل ممارسـة الفن بشـكل احترافي لـدى الفنانين الرواد.

ومـن أولئك الـرواد؛ برز اسـم الفنان يوسـف أحمـد جاها مـن مدينـة مكـة المكرمـة كأحـد الفنانيـن الذين أتيحت لهـم الفرصة بالمشاركة في المسـابقات والمعـارض والمحافـل الفنية محليـاً ودوليـاً، والذي حصل علـى العديد مـن الجوائز في مشـاركاته المحليـة والدولية. مـارس الفنـان جاها موهبتـه الفنيـة وعمـل علـى تثقيـف نفسـه بصرياً وفكرياً باسـتخدام أدوات فنية بسـيطة في مدينةٍ ينـدُر فيها وجود صالات ومعارض فنية ومحلات

motivating the formulation of the painting. It did not come in vain, and the painting was not a coincidence, but rather was based on a history and a profound artistic vision." In the context of his conversation with the writer Henry Heming; Jaha stated:

"I learn more from children than I learned in my academic studies in Riyadh. Being among them pushes me to act spontaneously without affectation, in addition to Makkah the place where I grew up, all of which had a great impact on my artistic production."

(Stapleton, London 2009)

In his early work, Jaha explored the interplay of shadows and light in his realist portraits. This experimentation with chiaroscuro continued into his later work, which became more impressionistic in style and depicted scenes of traditional homes in Makkah, folk dances, and the landscape of Al-Hada, a village 70 kilometers outside of Makkah. He used large brushstrokes when portraying dark skies, the earth, and the reflection of light on traditional buildings. Notable examples of this phase in his career include *Children of Stone* (1988), he exhibited at the Bangladesh Biennale in 1989, and *The Gulf Breakout and the Dance of the Birds* exhibited at the Saudi Contemporary Art Exhibition in Turkey in 1993.

Jaha's intimate knowledge of the alleys in Makkah is clear in his treatment of the rich visual elements of Makkah's motifs represented in the Hejazi *rawasheen* and *mashrabiyat*. His unique approach involved studying the details, dimensions, and proportions of these decorative elements, which he then incorporated into his own work. He added a personal touch by choosing shades of sky blue, gray, and beige, in addition to some bright colors in small details. This created a visual balance between the elements in composition, color, and space.

متخصصة لبيـع الأدوات الفنيـة الاحترافيـة فـي فتـرة السبعينيات والثمانينيـات. وفي أحـد لقاءاته مـع الكاتـب هنـري هيمينغ فـي لندن كمـا جاء في (ستابلتون، 2009م)؛ ذكر جاهـا إحـدى ذكرياتـه عندمـا رسـم والدته بأسـلوب مستوحى من إحدى لوحـات الفنان بيكاسـو التي رآها صدفة في إحدى المجلات، ويتذكر كيف تسـلل هاربـاً من والده الذي كان يسـتقبل الضيـوف فـي المجلس ليرسـم لوحته فـي إحـدى جنبـات شـلّم المنزل.

درس الفنـان يوسـف جاها في معهـد التربية الفنية فـي الرياض وحصل على درجـة البكالوريوس فـي التربيـة الفنيـة مـن جامعـة أم القرى فـي مكة المكرمـة عام 1983م، وعمـل معلمـاً للتربية الفنية فـي وزارة التعليـم من 1392هـ إلـى 1433هـ. ولمع نجمه بعد حصوله على الجائزة الأولى في المعرض العـام في دورته الثالثة في الرياض الـذي أقيم عام 1979م. كمـا لعـب جاهـا دوراً محوريـاً فـي تثقيف الجيـل التالـي مـن فناني مكة المكرمة، حيـث بادر بتنظيـم لقـاءات حوارية وإقامـة ورش فنية لأبناء مكة، وكان عضواً مؤسسـاً لمجموعة مكة التشكيلية التي بدأت فكرتها في مطلع التسـعينيات من القرن الماضـي واسـتمرت حتى عـام 2008م. تأثـر جاها بتنـوع الأنثروبولوجيا الثقافية والنسيج المجتمعي فـي مكـة المكرمة، فطـوّع عناصره البصريـة باحترام قدسـية المكان مـن منظور الفـن المعاصر.

تأصلت لـدى جاهـا احترافية الفـن الأكاديمي؛ فتدرج فـي تجاربـه الفنية متنقـلاً بيـن الاتجاهات الفنيـة العالميـة فـي عصر الحداثـة من الأسـلوب الواقعـي إلـى التأثيريـة ثم التجريديـة التعبيريـة، موظفـاً ثقافتـه البصرية المسـتوحاة مـن بيئتـه المحليـة المحيطة، لتأثـره بنظريات رسـوم الأطفال والعمـق الجمالـي فـي تلـك الرسـوم؛ وذلـك نظراً لاتصاله المباشـر بطلاب المرحلة الابتدائية كمعلم للتربيـة الفنية فـي مكة المكرمة لمـدة تزيـد عن الثلاثيـن عامـاً. ذكر الفنـان فـي مذكراتـه الخاصـة: «التجريـد فكـرة تتبلور تحـت ضغط رهيب مـن الأحاسيس والقوى الخفية المحفزة لصياغة اللوحة،

In a meeting with the writer Henry Hemming in London, Jaha recounted a memory from his formative years when he painted his mother in a style inspired by a Picasso work he came upon by chance in a magazine. He also remembered sneaking away from his father, who was hosting guests, to paint his portrait on one side of the staircase in the house (Stapleton, 2009, catalog by Edge of Arabia, London.).

Jaha's academic foundation in art was first cultivated at the Institute of Art Education in Riyadh, he later obtained a bachelor's degree in art education from Umm Al-Qura University in Makkah in 1983. His professional career started as an art teacher at the Ministry of Education, a role he held from 1971 to 2011. His popularity grew after winning the first prize in *The Third General Art Exhibition* in Riyadh, held in 1979. Jaha played an instrumental role in educating the next generation of Makkah's artists, initiating seminars and conducting artistic workshops. He was a founding member of the Makkah Fine Arts Group, an organization that was established in the early 1990s and continued until 2008. Influenced by the diverse cultural anthropology and social fabric of Makkah, Jaha adapted his visual elements, respecting the sanctity of the place through the lens of contemporary art.

Jaha's academic background in art formed the foundation of his professional career. He gradually progressed in his artistic experiences, navigating styles from realism to impressionism, then abstract expressionism. He employed a visual culture inspired by his surrounding local environment and influenced by analyzing children's drawings and the aesthetic depth therein. This stemmed from his time as a primary school art teacher in Makkah for over three decades. As the artist stated in his journals, "Abstraction is an idea that takes shape under terrible pressure from feelings and the hidden forces

فلم تـأت عبثاً ولم يكن الرسـم صدفة، بل اسـتندت إلـى تاريخ ورؤيـة فنيـة عميقة». وفي سـياق حديثه مـع الكاتـب هنـري هيمينغ؛ ذكـر جاها:

"أتعلـم مـن الأطفـال أكثـر ممـا تعلمتـه فـي دراستي الأكاديمية في الرياض، تواجدي بينهم يدفعنـي للتصـرف بشـكل تلقائـي دون تكلف، بالإضافة إلى مـكان إقامتي في مكـة المكرمة، كل ذلـك كان لـه تأثير كبيـر على إنتاجـي الفني."

(ستابلتون، 2009م)

تنـاول جاها فـي بداية حياته الفنية الأسـلوب الواقعـي في تجربة غنية جمعـت العتمة وومضات الضوء فـي صور شـخصية (البورتريـه). وظهرت في نهايـة التجربـة الواقعيـة تأثيـرات طفيفـة لضربات الفرشـاة وكانـت مدخـلاً لتبنـي أسـلوب المدرسـة التأثيريـة فـي الفنـون الجميلة، حيـث تميز جاهـا بضربات الفرشـاة العريضة في أعماله التـي تناولت المنـازل الشـعبية فـي مكـة المكرمـة، والرقصـات الشـعبية، والمناظـر الطبيعيـة لقُـرى الهَـدا التـي تبعـد نحـو 70 كيلومتـراً عـن مدينة مكـة المكرمة، وغيرهـا مـن الموضوعـات. وجمعـت التجربـة بين المساحات اللونية المعتمة للسماء والأرض بضربات عريضة وتركيز انعكاس الضوء على المباني الشـعبية والعناصـر الأخـرى كالتـي ظهـرت علـى اللوحـة المشـاركة في بينالي بنغلاديـش 1989م بعنـوان «أطفال الحجارة»، واللوحات المشـاركة في معرض الفـن السـعودي المعاصـر فـي تركيـا عـام 1987م بعنـوان «الانطلاقـة الخليجيـة، ورقصـة الطيـور». كما انعكسـت تأثيـرات الفرشـاة على تجربته التالية التـي تناولت النسـيج المعمـاري في مكـة المكرمة.

كان لحياة الفنان يوسـف جاها بيـن أزقة مكة المكرمة؛ أثـر واضـح فـي تنـاول العناصـر البصرية الغنيـة بالزخـارف المكيـة والمتمثلـة في الرواشـين والمشربيّات الحجازية على المباني، وتفردت تجربته -الرواشـين- بدراسـة تفاصيـل العناصـر الزخرفيـة والأبعاد والنِّسـب في الرواشين؛ فأضاف إليها طابعاً شـخصياً باختيار درجات الأزرق السـماوي والرمادي

hurufiyya-style works. Artist Nja Mahdaoui notes the peculiarity of this experience in Jaha's second solo exhibition catalog. He says:

"After all the artistic experiments and the search for the specificity of aesthetic dialogue, the painter Yousef Ahmad Jaha chose a kind of uniqueness with a plastic style and devised new methods. It may be useful and exciting at the same time to search for the formula that dominates his style, represented in his recent works, to scientifically establish Arab identity through a contemporary view."

The Bangladesh Biennale (1989) marked a turning point in his aesthetic fine art experimentation. He began to abstract elements of nature and multi-layered compositions (opaque and transparent) that explored the unique properties in the origin and nature of color. Broad, oblique lines expressed the overlapping clouds in the sky, while rainy clouds were rendered with childlike expressions. Building on his influential experience with brushstrokes and their studied movement to create a sense of visual movement linking the elements of nature in his painting. Jaha also employed expressive characteristics of children's drawings, such as transparency, deletion, exaggeration, flatness, and the horizon. This spontaneous style of drawing objects appeared in the works featured in his third solo exhibition in 2001, such as the abundant palm tree, rainy clouds, mountains, hills, and abstract portraits. In Jaha's fourth solo exhibition catalog (2005), Syrian critic Asaad Orabi commented on the symbolism of elements within Jaha's compositions:

It excelled in its expressive judgments, then the pure dialogues between the palm tree (the symbol of paradise) and its blessed clusters of dates, and between the swirling clouds (the blessing of

والبيج، بالإضافة إلى بعض الألوان الزاهية في بعض التفاصيل الصغيرة بالرواشين الحجازية؛ إليها أحدث التوازن البصري بين العناصر في التكوين واللون والمساحة. كما ظهرت ملامح المدرسة البنائية في تكوين الرواشين المتداخلة، قاصداً بها الفنان جذب المتلقي نحو التفاصيل الزخرفية ومبتعداً عن الأسلوب الواقعي في لوحات بانورامية، وملغياً المنظور الهندسي في بعض اللوحات. وكان ذلك الدافع نحو تبني تجريد العناصر في تجاربه الفنية (الحروفية والطبيعة). وهذا ما أكّده الفنان في كتيب معرضه الشخصي الثاني في عام 1996م بعنوان الطبيعة والإنسان والفن بأن:

"الهدف من المعرض ليس التجريد فقط، بل إن جوهره يكمن في البحث عن الذات وعن حقيقة التجريد من خلال الطبيعة والحرف لإغناء تجربتي الفنية."

كذلك في مذكرته بأن "التجريد ليس أحجية بقدر ما هو فكر تأملي متوقّد ينشد الاختزال."

وتفردت تجربة الحروفية العربية لدى جاها بتجريد الحرف العربي مستفيداً من رسومات طلّابه في دروس أسس التصميم والتي كان يقدمها ضمن منهج التربية الفنية في المرحلة الابتدائية، فظهرت التكوينات الطفولية كخلفية تربط الحروف المتناثرة، كما تفردت أشكال الحروف المجردة بانعكاس عفوية الطفل واحترافية الفنان في تكوين شكل الحرف، فنجد البنط العريض والسلخ العفوي في تشكيل الحروف المتداخلة مع الأخذ في الاعتبار توظيف بعض خصائص خط الثلث وبأسلوب تجريدي في رسم النقطة ورأس الألف.

وجاءت أهم أعماله الحروفية: الجدارية المنسوجة في مطار الملك خالد الدولي، وجدارية لمشروع تجميل مكة المكرمة، ولوحات مشروع تجميل مبنى الغرفة التجارية في الدمام، ومشروع تجميل مطعم شركة أرامكو السعودية. عكست تلك الأعمال تفرداً شكلياً وجمالياً دعا الكثير من النقاد إلى دراسة هذا المنتج لجاها، حيث ذكر

Constructivist elements are also evident in the composition of the overlapping windows. With which the artist sought to draw the viewer's attention to the decorative details rather than the realistic style of panoramic paintings. He also eliminated geometric perspective in some paintings, further emphasizing the decorative elements. The artist confirmed this in the catalog of his second solo exhibition *Nature, Human, and Art* (1996). He stated that:

> "The goal of the exhibition was not abstraction for its own sake, but rather its essence lies in the search for oneself and the truth of abstraction through nature and crafts."

The artist also pointed out in his journal that:

> "Abstraction is not a puzzle as much as it is an intense contemplative thought seeking reduction."

Jaha's experience with the hurufiyya style was unique in his abstraction of the Arabic letter. He drew inspiration from his students' drawings when he was teaching them the foundations of design. Childlike formations appeared as a background linking the scattered letters, the shapes of the abstract letters were unique, reflecting both the spontaneity of his students and the artist's professionalism in forming the shape of the letter. Jaha also incorporated some characteristics of the thuluth script into his abstract style by drawing the dot and the letter alif.

In 1983, his most important hurufiyya works included the woven mural at King Khalid International Airport in Riyadh for the Beautification and Improvement of Makkah in 2010, paintings for the Chamber of Commerce Building in Dammam, and a Saudi Aramco Restaurant Beautification Project. These works reflect a formal and aesthetic uniqueness that prompted many critics to study Jaha's

الفنان العالمـي نجا المهداوي فـي إحدى صفحات كتيب المعرض الشخصي الثاني للفنان يوسف جاها واصفـاً خصوصيـة هـذه التجربة:

كمـا أشـار الفنـان كذلـك فـي مذكرتـه بـأن "التجريـد ليـس أحجيـة بقـدر مـا هـو فكـر تأملـي متوقّـد ينشـد الاختـزال."

تفـردت تجربـة الحروفيـة العربيـة لـدى جاها بتجريد الحرف العربي مستفيداً من رسومات طلّابه في دروس أسـس التصميم والتي كان يقدمها ضمن منهج التربية الفنية في المرحلة الابتدائية، فظهرت التكوينات الطفولية كخلفية تربط الحروف المتناثرة، كمـا تفـردت أشـكال الحـروف المجـردة بانعـكاس عفوية الطفـل واحترافية الفنـان في تكوين شـكل الحرف، فنجـد البنط العريض والسـلخ العفوي في تشـكيل الحـروف المتداخلـة مع الأخذ فـي الاعتبار توظيـف بعـض خصائـص خـط الثلـث وبأسـلوب تجريدي في رسـم النقطـة ورأس الألف.

"بعـد كل التجـارب الفنيـة والبحـث عـن خصوصيـة الحـوار الجمالـي، اختـار الرسـام يوسـف أحمـد جاهـا نوعـاً مـن التفرد بنمط تشكيلي واستنباط أساليب جديدة. وقد يكون مـن المفيد والمثير في آن واحد أن نبحث عن الصيغـة التي يسـيطر عليهـا أسـلوبه المتمثل فـي أعماله الأخيـرة للتأصيـل العلمـي للهوية العربيـة مـن خـلال النظـرة المعاصرة."

يُمثل بينالي بنغلاديش الذي شـارك فيه الفنان يوسـف جاهـا فـي عـام 1989م؛ نقطة تحـول في تجربته التشـكيلية الجمالية وتناوله للعناصر البصرية في أعماله، فقد ظهر الاختزال البصري بتجريد عناصر الطبيعة، وتعـددت الطبقات (المعتمة والشـفافة) فـي المسـاحة الواحـدة مُحدِثةً خصائـص متفردة في أصـل اللون وكُنْـهِه. وتحولت الخطـوط المائلة العريضة والمعبرة عن تداخل السـحب في السـماء؛ إلى الغيـوم الممطرة ذات الخصائـص الطفولية في التعبيـر الفنـي، مستفيداً مـن تجربتـه التأثيرية في ضربات الفرشاة (الضبابية) وحركتها المدروسة والتي

merges with the background. Raindrops (twenty-six in total) fall toward the left of the painting, suggesting an easterly wind blowing in a desert. In his later works, the number of drops was reduced to seven, symbolizing the artist's belief in the generality of the goodness of nature and humanity. Jaha wrote in his diaries:

"This impact may lead us to life with all its contemporary components, and this is confirmed by the heavy cloud and raindrops quenching the earth's thirst. Or to the yard; Then civilizations continue by searching and excavating that antiquity. And nothing goes in vain. It is life within nature."

Jaha came up with the idea of a series of paintings entitled Nature's Talk after participating in the Bangladesh Biennale in 1989 and his visit to the accompanying exhibitions. It was Jaha's first visit to an international exhibition, where he met international artists and learned about diverse global experiences. This sparked his curiosity to explore the wider world of art from an intellectual perspective. In one of the Jaha's journal entries, he stated that: "The artist's attitude towards nature, either the image refers to something in nature (i.e. an image of reality) or the image refers to something in the artist's nature from the inside, and the third aspect is different because it creates his artistic compositions a creation that is unlike any other…", the Italian critic Giorgio Scato said about Jaha's work exhibited at the Sharjah International Biennial in 2001 (Makkah Fine Arts Group 2005, the fourth solo exhibition brochure).

Jaha began to include philosophical aspects into his abstract works, combining man and nature in one spirit. As stated in the book *Modern and Contemporary Saudi Art* (2015) "Art is humanity in which the glories of nature are united. It is flashes and

تمثـل الحركـة البصريـة الرابطة بين عناصـر الطبيعة في اللوحـة، كما وظف جاهـا الخصائـص التعبيرية لرسـوم الأطفـال كالشـفافية والحـذف والمبالغـة والتسطيح وخـط الأرض؛ فنجد الأسـلوب العفوي فـي رسـم العناصـر والتي ظهرت فـي أعمال معرضه الشـخصي الثالث في عـام 2001م، كالنخلة المثمرة والغيمـة الممطرة والجبـال والتـلال والتشـخيص المجرد، وحول ذلك ذكر الناقد السـوري أسعد عرابي فـي كتيب المعرض الشخصي الرابع في عام 2005م للفنـان جاهـا؛ حـول رمزية العناصر فـي أعماله:

«فهـي تفوقـت فـي أحكامهـا التعبيريـة، ثـم الحوارات الطهرانية بين النخلة (رمز الفردوس) وعناقيـد تمورها المباركة، وبين الغيمة المدارة (نعمة السـماء إزاء عطـش الأرض والغابة) ثم الخيمـة أو البيـت الريفي ثم الهيئة الملتبسـة بين شـكل المحراب والقباب الطينية، فالرسام يصـور بخطوط وألـوان زاهدة بالغـة الاختزال والشـفافية حتى يبدو تتابع المسـاحات وكأنه مرايـا متعاكسـة فـي مشـكاة متخلقة الأنـوار والأشـعة، ويتشـبع هـذا المشـهد الروحـي بإلماحـات عرفانيـة بالغـة الطهـارة باللـون الأبيـض، (لـون أرديـة الحجيـج والمعتمرين)».

ويتميـز الفنـان جاهـا بدراسـته التفصيليـة للعناصـر قبل تشـكيلها علـى اللوحة، فقد كان يجمع بعـض القصاصـات مـن رسـوم الأطفال فـي ملف خاص، مـع إضافة التعليقـات للتعبير عـن جمالية العفويـة التشـكيلية لـدى الطفـل، وذكـر فـي أحـد تعليقاتـه بالملـف:

«أنـا ورسـوم الأطفـال عشـق أزلـي مـن خلال تدريـس التربية الفنية فـي المرحلـة الابتدائية منـذ عـام 1392هـ وحتى عـام 1433هـ».

أضحت الغيمـة الممطـرة أيقونـة جاهـا المتفردة فـي أعمالـه التجريدية، ففي أحـد لقاءات الكاتب مع الفنان يوسـف جاها في مرسمه الخاص وجـد ملفـاً فيـه أكثر مـن 22 قصاصة من رسـوم الأطفـال تحـوي تقريباً 76 سـحابة وغيمة ممطرة

heaven in the face of the thirst of the earth and the forest), then the tent or the country house, then the ambiguous appearance between the shape of the mihrab and the clay domes. The artist draws with ascetic lines and colors that are extremely concise and transparent until the succession of spaces appears as if they are mirrors in a niche, creating lights and rays, and this spiritual scene is saturated with extremely pure mystical hints in white, the color of the robes of pilgrims."

Jaha is known for his detailed study of the elements before incorporating them into his paintings. He collected some clippings of students' drawings, adding comments on the artistic spontaneity of a child, he wrote:

"Children's drawings and I are an eternal love since teaching art education at the primary school since 1972 until 2012."

The rainy cloud became Jaha's icon in his abstract works. In one of Dr. Filfilan's meetings with Jaha in his private studio, he found a file with more than twenty-two snippets of children's drawings depicting approximately seventy-six clouds in different styles and shapes. Jaha studied and analyzed these drawings, reflecting their inspiration by incorporating the spontaneity of children into his own work. He experimented with different methods of coloring spaces and forming elements by directing the brush in several directions with deliberate movement. As a result, the rain clouds are sometimes depicted with a childlike layout, sometimes with colored spaces, and sometimes combining the two, creating transparency between the line and the space.

Rain clouds with abstract reductionism first appeared in his painting *Nature's Talk* for the 8th Cairo International Biennale in 2001. It features a zigzag line in the form of an arc, in which spontaneous brush strokes appear, and a color gradient below the line

بأساليب مختلفة وأشكال متنوعة، درسها الفنان وحللها بصرياً ليتناولها في أعماله باحترافية الفنان وعفوية الطفل في الرسم والتشكيل. كما قام بتأمل استخدام الأطفال لفرشاة الرسم ودراسة حركتها العشوائية في تكوين العناصر البصرية؛ ما انعكس على أسلوب الفنان في تلوين المساحات وتشكيل العناصر بتوجيه الفرشاة في عدة اتجاهات بحركة مدروسة، فنجد الغيمة الممطرة تارة بتخطيط طفولي وتارة بمساحات لونية وتارة بالجمع بينهما مُحدثاً الشفافية بين الخط والمساحة. وظهرت الغيمة الممطرة باختزالية التجريد لأول مرة في لوحته حوار الطبيعة المشاركة في بينالي القاهرة الدولي الثامن في عام 2001م، بخط متعرج على شكل قوس، تظهر فيه ضربات الفرشاة العفوية وبتدرج لوني أسفل الخط ليندمج مع لون الخلفية، وجاءت قطرات المطر المتساقطة (26 قطرة) متجهة نحو يسار اللوحة موحيةً بهبوب رياح شرقية في منطقة صحراوية، فيما تقلصت أعداد القطرات في مرحلة لاحقة من إنتاجه الفني حتى وصلت إلى سبع قطرات متساقطة من الغيمة؛ مختزلاً بها التعبير عن عمومية الخير على الطبيعة والإنسان. حيث كتب الفنان في مذكرته الخاصة:

"هذا الأثر قد يقودنا إلى الحياة بكل مقوماتها المعاصرة، ويؤكد ذلك الغيمة المدرارة وحبات المطر تروي عطش الأرض، أو إلى الفناء؛ عندها تتواصل الحضارات عن طريق البحث والتنقيب عن ذلك الأثر، ولا شيء يذهب هدراً، إنها الحياة داخل الطبيعة."

وبدأ جاها بتضمين الجانب الفلسفي في أعماله التجريدية بالجمع بين الإنسان والطبيعة في روح واحدة. فقد جاء في كتاب الفن السعودي الحديث والمعاصر 2015م عن الفنان جاها: «الفن هو الإنسانية التي التحمت فيها أمجاد الطبيعة، وهو ومضات ومهرجان من طبقات الألوان والشكل والأبعاد وخطوط الانحناء التي تتلوّى وتتجمع وتتقاطع وتتكسر لتطفئ نار وظمأ الأرض العطشى». وكتب جاها في مذكرته الخاصة:

Jaha included rain dropping from clouds and quenching the thirsty earth. He formed elements by drawing faces inspired by studying more than forty-four clippings of children's drawings, which included more than 274 drawings the artist analyzed from his own collection. Orabi noted in Jaha's sixth solo exhibition catalog (2019):

"... he sees things from above, from their inner and outer sides, which is the difference between sight and insight (according to the dialectic of Abu Hamid al-Ghazali) and the dialectic of (transcendence and simile) corresponding in Western depiction to the duality of (abstraction and personification). for Jaha, the personification (like faces) of abstraction and abstraction converges together."

In the midst of Jaha's recent—2017 to 2024—experience of nature and man, he addresses one of the characteristics of young students' drawings that appear in his collection of clippings: that of combining surfaces and solids in one space. This characteristic reflects a child's lack of adherence to a specific angle in the drawing, as Abdul Muttalib Al-Quraiti pointed out in his *Introduction to the Psychology of Children's Drawings*. A child moves around an object to see it from several different angles, they choose a perspective for the object they draw and add it to the perspective they drew in a previous session, combining them into one form. Some authors refer to this characteristic as "exemplarity," meaning situations in which the outstanding characteristics and features of the painted object appear in the clearest and most complete possible picture from the child's cognitive point of view.

In some of his later works, Jaha combined the human-eye perspective on the horizon line with the bird's eye perspective. He used this technique to depict abstract elements of nature and simplified representational forms, as well as geometric and suggestive color

"أعمالي تُشكل جزءاً حيوياً من شخصيتي، ونوعاً من الإيمان والثقة والفطرة التي تشكلت منها مفاهيمي وثقافتي، ومنها أيضاً تشكلت المفردات الأولى للطبيعة. ومضات وطبقات من الألوان والأشكال والمساحات والخطوط تخدش الفرشاة ما شكلته سابقاً. طمس خطوط ومساحات وإنشاء أخرى موازية تنحني تتجمع تتقاطع تتكسر، نقاط تتناثر، تتأثر بجاذبية الغيمة (نعمة السماء) وحبات المطر تتحرك وتتشكل لتروي عطش الأرض."

تميزت شخصية الفنان جاها بالتواضع والانفتاح على الآخر، بالإضافة إلى ذكائه الاجتماعي وتقبُّل الرأي وحسن الإنصات والمبادرة في تثقيف الفنانين الناشئين. وأضحى ذلك بتأثر بعض الفنانين من الجيل التالي بتقمص شخصيته واتباع أسلوبه المتفرد في تناول عناصر الطبيعة بأسلوب تجريدي. ويؤكد ذلك الثقفي 2022م في بحثه بعنوان التّناص البصري في أعمال التشكيليين السعوديين، فقد أشار إلى تعبير الفنان يوسف جاها في إحدى لوحاته بتسجيل لحظة لمنظر طبيعي بأسلوب تجريدي اختزالي يكاد يصل إلى التجريد الكلي الذي ينقل اللوحة إلى التجريد اللوني ولكنه يُبقي المشاهد على تواصل مع اللوحة من خلال عناصر الطبيعة، وقد تناص أحد الفنانين تناصّاً كليّاً مع لوحة الفنان جاها؛ وذلك باستعارة العناصر المرئية التشكيلية لأعماله، كما ظهر التّناص في أنماط عدة مثل: التضمين في أغلب العناصر التكوينية للوحة، والتوسيع في بعضها الآخر.

تناول جاها التشخيص المختزل والمتضمن في ثناياه قطرات الخير من الغيمة الممطرة على الأرض الظمأى، فتشكلت عناصره برسم الوجوه المستوحاة من عفوية الأطفال في التعبير، وذلك من خلال دراسة أكثر من 44 قصاصة لرسوم الأطفال تضمنت أكثر من 274 رسمة تشخيصية، حللها الفنان وعلق عليها في ملفه الخاص. فقد ذكر الناقد أسعد عرابي في كتيب المعرض الشخصي السادس للفنان جاها في عام 2019م:

a festival of layers of colors, shapes, dimensions, and bending lines that twist, gather, intersect, and break to quench the fire and thirst of the thirsty earth." Jaha wrote in his journal:

"My works form a vital part of my personality, a kind of faith, trust, and instinct from which my concepts and culture were formed, and from which the first vocabulary of nature was also formed. Flashes and layers of colors, shapes, spaces, and lines scratch the brushes over what they previously formed. Blurring lines and spaces and creating parallel ones that bend, come together, intersect, and break points scattered, affected by the gravity of the cloud (the blessing of the sky) and raindrops moving and forming to quench the earth's thirst."

Jaha's personality was characterized by humility, openness, and social intelligence. He is accepting of opinions, good at listening, and has developed initiatives to help educate emerging artists. This influenced some artists from the next generation to follow in his lead when dealing with elements of nature in an abstract manner. Al-Thaqafi confirms this in his research "Visual Intertextuality Artworks of Saudi Artists." He refers to Yousef Jaha's expression in one of his paintings, from Nature's Talk series, which records a moment from a landscape in a reductive abstract style that almost reaches total abstraction. This shifts the painting toward color abstraction, but Jaha keeps the audience's connection to the painting through the elements of nature. Other emerging artists have completely intertextualzed themselves with Jaha's painting by borrowing his visual elements. Intertextuality also appeared in several patterns, such as the inclusion in most of the compositional elements of the painting and expansion in others.

"يرى الأشياء من أعلى، من طرفيها الباطن والظاهر، هو الفرق بين البصر والبصيرة وفق جدلية أبي حامد الغزالي وجدلية (التنزيه والتشبيه) المقابلة في التصوير الغربي لثنائية (التجريد والتشخيص). لدى جاها يتقارب التشخيص (مثل الوجوه) من التنزيه والتجريد معا."

وفي خِضَمّ تجربة الطبيعة والإنسان لدى الفنان جاها، تناول في بعض أعماله الأخيرة في الفترة من 2017م وحتى 2024م إحدى خصائص رسوم الأطفال التي ظهرت في الملف الخاص بقصاصات رسوم طلابه، وهي الجمع بين المسطحات والمجسمات في حيز واحد، وهذه الخاصية هي من مظاهر عدم التزام الطفل بزاوية معينة في الرسم، كما أشار إليها القريطي 2001م بأن الطفل يلجأ إلى التعبير عن الأشياء كما لو كان يدور حولها ليراها من عدة زوايا مختلفة، وفي كل دورة ينتقي وجهاً للشيء الذي يرسمه ليضيفه إلى الوجه الذي انتقاه في دورة سابقة، ويقوم بالتأليف بينها في شكل واحد. وتسمى هذه الخاصية عند بعض المؤلفين بتخيّر الأوضاع المثالية أي الأوضاع التي تظهر معها الخصائص والمميزات البارزة في الشيء المرسوم في أوضح وأكمل صورة ممكنة من وجهة نظر الطفل المعرفية.

جمع جاها في بعض أعماله الأخيرة بين منظور عين الإنسان في خط الأفق ومنظور عين الطائر؛ في تناول عناصر الطبيعة المجردة والتشخيص المختزل، فظهرت المساحات اللونية الهندسية والموحية إلى تقسيمات الأراضي الزراعية والأحياء السكنية في بيئة ما، كما لو كان يشاهدها من نافذة الطائرة المحلقة فوق المدينة استعداداً للهبوط، وذلك بالتزامن مع عناصر الطبيعة في خط الأفق كالأشجار والجبال والتلال والغيمة الممطرة بأسلوب تجريدي يجمع بين عفوية الطفل وتمكّن الفنان المحترف. وتناول الناقد أسعد عرابي فلسفة الجمالية لدى جاها في أعماله الأخيرة قائلاً:

"وفي البلاغة الإيجاز، أو النفري حين يقول: كلما اتسعت الرؤيا ضاقت العبارة. هي النزعة

References

Ali, Wijdan. (2002). *From the Ocean to the Gulf, Beyond the Horizon, Modern Arab Art*. The Permanent Collection of the Jordan National Gallery of Fine Arts. Amman, Hashemite Kingdom of Jordan: The Royal Society of Fine Arts.

Al-Thaqafi, Abdullah (2022). "Visual Intertextuality Artworks of Saudi Artists, an analytical study." *Zarqa Journal for Research and Studies in Humanities*. 22(1) 110-128.

Al-Quraiti, Abdul Muttalib. (2001). *Introduction to the Psychology of Children's Drawings*. Cairo, Egypt: Dar ElFiker Elarabi. 2nd ed.

Choudhury, S., Jinnah, E., and Shahidullah M. (1989). *Asian Art Biennale Bangladesh*. Dhaka, Bangladesh: Bangladesh Shilpakala Academy.

General Presidency of Youth Welfare. (1987). *Saudi Contemporary Art Exhibition in Turkey*. Riyadh, Kingdom of Saudi Arabia: Middle East Press.

International Fine Arts Gallery. (2005). *Yousef Jaha. Jeddah, Saudi Arabia: Booklet for the fourth solo exhibition*. International Fine Arts Gallery.

Makkah Fine Arts Group (2005) *The Body of Nature*. Makkah, Kingdom of Saudi Arabia: Fourth solo exhibition brochure.

Mono Gallery. (2024). Retrieved on March 4, 2024, from https://www.instagram.com/monogallery/?hl=ar

Nawar, Ahmed. (2001). *The Eighth Cairo International Biennale*. Cairo, Egypt: Ministry of Culture - Fine Arts

Sector, Central Administration for Artistic Services for Museums and Exhibitions.

Orabi, Asaad. (2019). *Mada*. Riyadh, Saudi Arabia: Booklet for the sixth solo exhibition by Yousef Jaha. Mono Gallery.

Personal files and journals of Yousef Jaha. (Unpublished clippings).

Rochan Gallery (1996). *Artist Yousef Jaha*. Jeddah, Kingdom of Saudi Arabia: Rochan Gallery.

Stapleton, S. (2009). *Edge of Arabia, Contemporary Art from Saudi Arabia*, London 2008, Venice 2009. Riyadh, Saudi Arabia: Saudi Arabia Ministry of Culture and Information.

The Al-Mansouria Foundation (2015). *Modern and Contemporary Saudi Art*. Jeddah, Kingdom of Saudi Arabia: The Al-Mansouria Foundation for Culture and Creativity.

الاختزالية البسيطة المسطحة المقتصرة على بُعدين فقط، والتي استعار بساطتها الفن المعاصر، ابتداء من هنري ماتيس ومقصوصاته الورقية الملونة، بما فيه تعددية مواقع النظر ومصادر الإضاءة، واعتماد منظور الطائر العنقاء أو السيمرغ الذي يسكن القبة الفلكية..."

سيطر الفنان يوسف جاها على تناغم الروح بين الإنسان والأرض والطبيعة، منطلقاً من بيئته المقدسة مكة المكرمة بأزقّتها المتداخلة إلى مجابهة الفن العالمي المتشعب شرقاً وغرباً، سالكاً طرقاً مختلفة في كل تجربة يخوضها، مرتحلاً بين ثنايا الألوان والخطوط، ومحافظاً على بساطة الطفولة العفوية وعمق التعقيد في الفن. ويشير جاها في مذكرته الخاصة:

"ويبقى الأثر هنا إشارة إلى سكون أو موت أو حياة، تسير بفعل اللاوعي تتحرر من قيود الشكل، ومنها انطلقت إشارات ورموز أخرى تنبع مباشرة، فالطاقة مركزة، ومتعة هذا العمل لابد وأن تأتي من الداخل، حيث تقودك في النهاية إلى قراءة مباشرة ومن ثم تدخلك إلى تفاصيل التأمل (حوار الطبيعة – جسد الطبيعة) وعندها لا تحمل بدايات أو نهايات إلا في فضاء الأمكنة ونبض الطبيعة."

spaces to divide agricultural lands and residential neighborhoods. It is as if the viewer is looking out the window of an airplane flying over the city in preparation for landing, while also seeing elements of nature on the horizon line, such as trees, mountains, hills, and rainy clouds. This style combines the spontaneity of a child with the mastery of a professional artist. Orabi addressed Jaha's recent aesthetic philosophy commenting:

"... and (in the rhetoric of brevity) or Al-Nafari when he says: (the wider the vision, the narrower the phrase). It is a flat reductionism (minimalism) limited to only two dimensions. Minimalism borrowed from contemporary art, starting with Henri Matisse and his colored paper scissors. Including the multiplicity of viewing locations and lighting sources, and the adoption of the perspective of the bird (Phoenix or semerg) inhabiting the planetarium."

Jaha has mastered the harmonious interplay between humanity, earth, and nature. Emanating from his sacred environment of Makkah, with its intricate web of alleys, he confronted the international art scene by exploring diverse artistic paths. His journey weaves through the folds of colors and lines, preserving the spontaneous simplicity of childhood while embracing the of complexities of art. Jaha wrote in his journal:

"The effect here remains a signal of stillness, death or life, driven by the action of the unconscious, freed from the constraints of form. And from there he started. Other signs and symbols emanate directly, the energy is concentrated. The pleasure of this work must come from within, as it eventually leads you to a direct reading and then introduces you to the details of meditation (Nature Talk-the body of nature) and then it has no beginnings or endings except in the space of places and the pulse of nature."

المراجع

الثقفي، عبدالله (2022). التناصّ البصري في أعمال التشكيليين السعوديين، دراسة نقدية تحليلية. مجلة الزرقاء للبحوث والدراسات الإنسانية. 22(1)، 110-128.

روشان غاليري. (1996). الفنان يوسف جاها. جدة، المملكة العربية السعودية: روشان غاليري.

الرئاسة العامة لرعاية الشباب. (1987). معرض الفن السعودي المعاصر بتركيا. الرياض، المملكة العربية السعودية: مطابع الشرق الأوسط.

صالة العالمية للفنون الجميلة. (2005). يوسف جاها. جدة، المملكة العربية السعودية: كتيب المعرض الشخصي الرابع.

مجموعة مكة التشكيلية (2005). جسد الطبيعة. مكة المكرمة، المملكة العربية السعودية: مطوية المعرض الشخصي الرابع.

عرابي، أسعد. (2019). مدى. الرياض، المملكة العربية السعودية: كتيب المعرض الشخصي السادس للفنان يوسف جاها. مونو غاليري.

علي، وجدان. (2002). معرض من المحيط إلى الخليج، فما وراء الأفق، فن عربي حديث. المجموعة الدائمة للمتحف الوطني الأردني للفنون الجميلة. عمّان، المملكة الأردنية الهاشمية: الجمعية الملكية للفنون الجميلة.

القريطي، عبدالمطلب. (2001). مدخل إلى سيكولوجية رسوم الأطفال. القاهرة، جمهورية مصر العربية: دار الفكر العربي. ط2.

مؤسسة المنصورية. (2015). الفن السعودي الحديث والمعاصر. جدة، المملكة العربية السعودية: مؤسسة المنصورية للثقافة والإبداع.

مونو غاليري. (2024). مسترجع بتاريخ 4 مارس 2024م من https://www.instagram.com/monogallery/?hl=ar

نوار، أحمد. (2001). بينالي القاهرة الدولي الثامن. القاهرة، جمهورية مصر العربية: وزارة الثقافة – قطاع الفنون التشكيلية، الإدارة المركزية للخدمات الفنية للمتاحف والمعارض.

ملفات ومذكرات شخصية للفنان يوسف جاها. (قصاصات غير منشورة).

شودري وجناة وشهيد الله (1989). بينالي الفن الآسيوي في بنغلاديش. دكا، بنغلاديش: أكاديمية شيلباكالا في بنغلاديش.

ستابلتون، (2009). Edge of Arabia، الفن المعاصر من المملكة العربية السعودية، لندن 2008، البندقية 2009. الرياض، المملكة العربية السعودية: وزارة الثقافة والإعلام.

Yearning for Rain
Yousef Jaha

May 26 - September 19, 2024
Prince Faisal bin Fahd Arts Hall
Riyadh, Saudi Arabia

Curators
Shadin Albulaihed,
Assistant Curator at Misk Art Institute
Madiha Sebbani,
Curator at Misk Art Institute

Art Direction
Amerah Altufail,
Art Production Director at Misk Art Institute

Exhibition Designers
Alanood Alkhaldi,
Exhibition Designer at Misk Art Institute
Badr Zabarah,
Senior Exhibition Designer at Misk Art Institute

Translations
Abdulrahman Sidi,
Senior Editor at Misk Art Institute

Authors
Shadin Albulaihed
Madiha Sebbani
Dr. Mohammad Filfilan
Basma Alshathry,
Director of Curatorial Department and Chief Curator

Copyediting
Ethar Alfaqeeh,
Copywriter at Misk Art Institute

Special thanks to the artist, galleries, collectors and institutions for their invaluable contributions.

تحــرّي المطــر
يوسـف جاها

26 مايو - 19 سبتمبر 2024
صالة الأمير فيصل بن فهد للفنون
الرياض، المملكة العربية السعودية

القيّمون الفنيون
شادن البليهد،
قيم فني مساعد في معهد مسك للفنون
مديحة صباني،
قيم فني في معهد مسك للفنون

التوجه الإبداعي
أميرة الطفيل،
مدير الإخراج الفني في معهد مسك للفنون

تصميم المعرض
العنود الخالدي،
مصمم معارض في معهد مسك للفنون
بدر زباره،
مصمم معارض أول في معهد مسك للفنون

الترجمة
عبدالرحمن سيدي،
محرر أول في معهد مسك للفنون

المؤلفون
شادن البليهد
مديحة صباني
دكتور محمد فلفلان
بسمة الشثري،
مدير عام إدارة التقييم الفني وكبير القيمين الفنيين

التدقيق اللغوي
إيثار الفقيه،
كاتب محتوى في معهد مسك للفنون

شكر خـاص للفنـان والجاليريـات والمقتنيـن والمؤسسـات علـى مسـاهماتهم القيمـة.

Book Design and Layout
-scope Ateliers

English Proofreading
Zeina Assaf

First edition, 2024
© Kaph Books, 2024
© Misk Art Institute, 2024

ISBN: 978-614-8035-85-2

Printed in October 2024

Published by

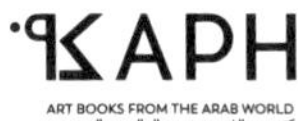

www.kaphbooks.com

Distribution
NORTH AMERICA - LATIN AMERICA - ASIA - AUSTRALIA
ARTBOOK | D.A.P.
75 Broad Street, Suite 630
New York, NY 10004
www.artbook.com

FRANCE - SWITZERLAND - BELGIUM - LUXEMBOURG
Les Presses du Réel
35 rue Colson,
21000 Dijon, France
www.lespressesdureel.com

REST OF EUROPE
Idea Books
Nieuwe Herengracht 11
1011 RK Amsterdam, The Netherlands
www.ideabooks.nl

MIDDLE EAST
CIEL BOOK DISTRIBUTION
Al Manara Road, Al Quoz 1, P.O.Box 282005
Dubai United Arab Emirates
www.ciel.me

تصميم الكتاب وتنسيقه
-سكوب أتلييه

المراجعة اللغوية العربية
محمد حمدان

الطبعة الأولى، 2024
© كتب كيف، 2024
© معهد مسك للفنون، 2024

ردمك: 978-614-8035-85-2

طُبع في أكتوبر 2024

النشر من قبل

www.kaphbooks.com

التوزيع
أمريكا الشـمالية - أمريكا اللاتينية - آسيا - أستراليا
ARTBOOK | D.A.P.
75 شارع برود، جناح 630
نيويورك، نيويورك 10004
www.artbook.com

فرنسا - سويسرا - بلجيكا - لوكسمبورغ
Les Presses du Réel
35 شارع كولسون،
21000 ديجون، فرنسا
www.lespressesdureel.com

بقية أوروبا
Idea Books
نيووي هيرنغراخت 11
RK 1011 أمستردام، هولندا
www.ideabooks.nl

الشرق الأوسط
CIEL BOOK DISTRIBUTION
شارع المنارة، القوز 1، ص.ب 282005
دبي، الإمارات العربية المتحدة
www.ciel.me